BEING SEEN

BEING SEEN

One Deafblind
Woman's Fight
to End Ableism

Elsa Sjunneson

Tiller Press

New York   London   Toronto   Sydney   New Delhi

TILLER PRESS

An Imprint of Simon & Schuster, Inc.
1230 Avenue of the Americas
New York, NY 10020

First Tiller Press hardcover edition October 2021

TILLER PRESS and colophon are registered
trademarks of Simon & Schuster, Inc.

For information about special discounts for bulk purchases, please
contact Simon & Schuster Special Sales at 1-866-506-1949
or business@simonandschuster.com.

The Simon & Schuster Speakers Bureau can bring authors to your live
event. For more information or to book an event, contact the
Simon & Schuster Speakers Bureau at 1-866-248-3049
or visit our website at www.simonspeakers.com.

Interior design by Laura Levatino

Manufactured in the United States of America

1   3   5   7   9   10   8   6   4   2

Library of Congress Cataloging-in-Publication Data has been applied for.

ISBN 978-1-9821-5237-6
ISBN 978-1-9821-5241-3 (ebook)

To everyone who said "you can't" "you shouldn't" "please, don't."

I can. I should. I did.

Thank you for teaching me to be stubborn.

And for Deafblind women everywhere, living in liminal space.

Contents

BEING SEEN

Author's Note

With the exception of historical and public figures, all names have been changed. Personal conversations and events in this book have been constructed from memory to the best of my ability.

CONTENT WARNING: This book contains explicit depictions of ableism; school bullying; sexual assault and abuse and references to caregiver murder; police brutality; emotional abuse; physical abuse. For detailed content warnings for each chapter, please visit the author's website.

1.

The Building Blocks
of Blindness

Hi, I'm Elsa.

Everyone has always assumed that I will die young. At this point in my midthirties, I'm no longer convinced they're right. I spent a long time imagining how I was going to die. It was always an accident. The people who love me probably think about it more than I do. I see it in their faces.

I understand. They're not wishing for my death; in fact, they're dreading it. But as anybody who cares about me knows, I'm going to continue running off and living my life exactly the way I want to, and I won't let something as benign as the body I was born in stop me.

I get portents of my death every once in a while. Maybe this time I won't notice when a car turns on a red. Maybe I won't hear someone shouting to watch where I'm going. I've taken harrowing falls, narrowly escaped speeding cars, gone swimming where I shouldn't. I've attempted to live my life like a nondisabled person, sometimes to a dangerous degree. There are things that stop me, of course, but I don't wake up in the morning wondering what's going to kill me because of my sight or hearing that day. I've moved fully into the realm of the living.

That's because I've learned how to survive in a body that wasn't intended for the world I live in. I'm certain of almost every step I take, certain that my adaptive aids will carry me through. Until 2020, when I stopped being able to control my environment in the ways that keep me alive. When all my adaptive aids failed in the span of four weeks. When I had to reconfigure my understanding of my body.

It was four weeks into the shelter-in-place order in Seattle, Washington, when one of my hearing aids failed me. The important one, of course. Three days before that, my guide dog broke his toe while playing with the neighbor dog. I had recently moved back to the Central District, where I had grown up, so at least I knew the neighborhood, but it wasn't the house I'd lived in before.

For the first time in a decade, I was actively Deafblind again. Stripped bare of my adaptive aids, I had to start asking myself some difficult questions. How comfortable was I walking with a white cane to the audiologist without working hearing aids, instead of asking my mom or my neighbor to take me? Could I cross the street by myself, without my dog?

I had to remember what it was like to be Deafblind without

assistance, and I quickly realized that it was the perfect time to remember what it is that makes me a Deafblind person at all.

It is the measure of distance, between me and the nondisabled people who surround me, who sharply define the boundaries of my world. Not my body. Not merely nondisabled society at large, but individuals who make specific decisions that leave me stranded in their wake.

It is the fact that I cannot effectively communicate when someone is across a silent room, with no audible distractions, without a hearing aid. Even with aids, add a plexiglass barrier between me and a cashier (who also happens to be wearing a mask) and I'm sunk.

It is the fact that without a guide dog, I feel disconnected, my body seeking anchors. I can still see, but perception is not the same thing as seeing sharply into the distance.

But it doesn't have to be that way. I *feel* that way because of what I have been told is expected of my body and what the norms are for human interaction and ability.

And, most important, because of what people expect when they hear the word "Deafblind."

Hi. My name is Elsa R. Sjunneson. I'm Deafblind.

What do you think being Deafblind means?

If you're a nondisabled, fully sighted, fully hearing person, you may have some very specific ideas of what Deafblindness looks like. Perhaps you've read about Helen Keller, the most famous historical example. Or you might have read Haben Girma's book. Or maybe you've actually heard of Laura Bridgman.

If you're disabled (either invisibly or visibly, via physical or mental or other means), you may also have some perceptions that need altering. After all, the disability community is not a mono-lith.[1]

If you *have* met someone who is Deafblind, I want you to think about what they looked like, what adaptive devices they used, how they adapted to the world around them.

If you haven't, I want you to imagine it.[2]

Can't picture it? Can't picture me? Let's try an exercise of the imagination.

What does a blind person look like to you? Do they wear dark glasses? Carry a white cane or have a guide dog? Are their eye sockets empty, or does a cloudy cataracted pair of eyes live within their ocular sphere? Do you know? Are they wearing sunglasses or prescription lenses?

What does a D/deaf person look like? Can you even tell if they're D/deaf until they turn up their hearing aids, or until they sign?

Okay, now flip to the back of this book. Take a look at the head-shot on the back cover. I'll wait.

Do I look Deafblind to you?

I know.

I don't, do I?

---

1   Some members of the disability community won't even agree with this book! I expect that!

2   Yes, this book will be dispensing with the fourth wall forthwith. Please find it somewhere in the literary wreckage.

I look at the camera, not away from it. I have one gray eye with a pupil and the other is clouded by a cataract, aqua blue and white. I wear glasses, they're stylish and frame my face well.[3] My hearing aids are pink and gray and don't hide behind my hair. My makeup is done—I'm wearing deep pink lipstick, a white and black striped silk blouse and leather vest. Vintage chic, and yes I styled myself.

I get it. To you this doesn't look like a Deafblind person. I'm often stopped in the street, told that I look great "for a blind person." I'm often asked if my caretakers have dressed me (my ex-husband Gatsby even received compliments for it!).

The problem is that no one really knows what disability looks like, because you'd have to be able to identify a million different degrees of blindness or deafness at first glance. And that would require magic, or at least technology far beyond what we have today.

Instead, you have to trust people—and for some reason, nondisabled people don't seem inclined to trust the disabled. Whether it is suspicion about *how* disabled we really are, or doubt about whether we are "safe" to be out by ourselves, many of the interactions between disabled people and the nondisabled public are deeply fraught.

People are afraid of disability. In 2014, *Star Trek* alumnus George Takei posted a meme on his wildly popular Facebook fan

---

3 Right now they are purple and gold, vintage-style and effortlessly quirky but feminine. Maybe they'll be something else when you read this.

page. It was an image of a wheelchair user standing up to grab a bottle of liquor from a high shelf. The caption read: "There has been a miracle in the alcohol isle [*sic*]."[4] Takei was instantly called out by disability activists across the internet, reminding him that disabilities are not a monolith, that there are degrees of difference.

It's supposed to be funny, but underneath the humor, there's a very real danger. Nondisabled people frequently appoint themselves the disability police, approaching strangers who don't look disabled enough, questioning whether they really need that parking placard, that wheelchair, that guide dog.

This is why I need to get you on the same page with me before we can move forward. When I share my story you're going to need to trust me and, more important, believe me.

So we've talked about what you think a Deafblind person looks like. Now, what do you think a Deafblind person can do? Does your list include the following?

- Skiing double black diamonds.
- Hiking Arthur's Seat.
- Fencing saber.
- Competing in Lindy Hop.
- Winning literary awards.

---

4 Bryan Alexander, "George Takei: Facebook 'Mistakes' Part of Life," *USA Today*, August 23, 2014, https://www.usatoday.com/story/tech /personal/2014/08/23/george-takei-facebook-wheelchair/14467837/.

- Independently traveling internationally.
- Moving across the country alone.
- Being married.
- Speaking multiple languages.
- Using footnotes with indiscriminate glee.[5]

If you didn't think of any of those things, think again. Because I've done all of them. I speak five languages.[6] I've been married. I've moved across countries, won multiple international awards, and even traveled abroad by myself (the guide dog doesn't count because he's an adaptive aid[7]).

Many would perceive blind and deaf people as lost and alone, set adrift by their disabilities, unable to fully participate in the world at large.

And there is some truth to it. We are often left out. But that's not because we cannot participate. It's because society has chosen not to adapt to us, to our ways of living, communicating, and adapting.

---

5   Braille does, by the way, use footnotes. They are in line instead of at the bottom of the page. So if you were wondering how exactly other blind people were going to access this snark—I promise it's right there waiting.

6   English native; French near fluent (when immersed); Swedish and German badly; American Sign Language and Hebrew are the ones I'm learning. I can read Latin, too!

7   Yeah, I know, it's weird to think of a dog as a medical device, but here we are.

It's not that I've chosen to be adrift or even want to be. It's that society presents me with a binary choice: adapt the way we expect you to, look and dress and behave accordingly, or be cut out. If I'm seen as too different, I risk losing access to the things I need to live.

That's why, when you look at me, you have trouble seeing a Deafblind person. You've been misled.

For example, you've been told that Deafblind people do not speak orally and that we are only able to communicate via interpreters or through sign language. But here I am, a Deafblind woman who rarely, if ever, stops talking. A Deafblind woman who can perform Shakespeare and who holds National Forensic League[8] titles. Not only can I talk, I can talk circles around some very smart people. With a smile on my face.

You've been told that Deafblind people cannot live alone, but here I am in a house by myself. You've been told we cannot be educated, but I have a master's in women's history, and Haben Girma graduated from Harvard Law.[9]

You've been told that we wear hearing aids but don't hear much, that we must sign with our hands or use interpreters. You've been told that we exist in a perpetual state of darkness despite the fact that most blind people have some light perception at the very least—and many have more than that.

---

8 Now called the National Speech & Debate Association.

9 Haben Girma, *Haben: The Deafblind Woman Who Conquered Harvard Law* (New York: Twelve, 2019).

So let's flip the script for a second.

What do you think a sighted person looks like? What about a hearing person? What can they do? Can they ski? Can they hike? Have they traveled by themselves? Have they gotten married? *How would you know?*

There.

That moment when you sit back, take a breath, and realize that a disabled person may be as different from a fellow disabled person as anyone else—just as all nondisabled people are different from one another.

You don't know.

No one does.

So why does society insist on a binary system for defining blindness and deafness?

Because our culture relentlessly seeks two things: simplicity of understanding and the ability to sort into groups.

Disability is a broad category, containing millions of individuals, yet we treat it as a monolith, even today.

———

I was born in 1985, in New York City, to queer parents who wanted me. I was born with working eyes but without reasonably functioning ears or a heart that worked terribly efficiently. My parents went from excitedly counting my fingers and toes to figuring out how to manage a Deafblind baby (though they wouldn't use that word at the time). They would fight with doctors over treating me as human, and they would navigate a medical system, an educational system, and a social system that didn't really know what to do with me.

They would raise me in nondisabled society. I would not learn American Sign Language (ASL) or braille, nor would I be in special education classrooms. I would not go to Deaf or blind school, nor would I have a lot of blind friends. I wouldn't grow up steeped in Deaf culture,[10] so I would have to forge my own path to adulthood with a disability.

This book is more or less about how I got to thirty-five: with a handful of scars, some emotional trauma, and a healthy appreciation for the art form known as snark.

There were doctors who told me I wouldn't make it to thirty-five. Hell, there were doctors who told me I wouldn't make it to thirty. They made all kinds of predictions about how my body would betray me.

Even without the doctors, there was another specter that hung over my childhood: there was no one to look up to and see what my life might be like. Sure, there was Helen Keller, but Helen Keller was more Deafblind than I am. She went to Perkins.[11] The blind and Deaf women that I saw in books (only a handful) barely resembled me. The blind and Deaf men were worse, and the gender binary was such a strongly enforced thing in the 1990s that it wouldn't have mattered anyway. I didn't want to be compared to a boy. Why were the men worse? Because they conformed to mas-

---

10 Most children of hearing adults don't, but it is worth noting.

11 The oldest blind boarding school in the country!

culine stereotypes that were about overcoming, and none of them had been born like I was.

In order to get here, I had to fight the dragons of ableism, internalized ableism, and more. I've made a lot of mistakes. I've been selfish when I should have been kind, I've been a hermit when I should have reached out. I've broken hearts and been impulsive and fallen short of my best self. But I've tried my hardest to be the kind of person I wanted to be.

In order to do that, I had to forgive myself for the body that I live in.

I had to become comfortable with the fact that I was the only Deafblind person I knew (until I wasn't; now I know several more). But it shouldn't have to be this way. So many people are being left behind—they don't see themselves reflected in the stories that we tell or in the society we choose to erect.

Nondisabled people, buckle up: this book might be a bit of a ride.

Disabled people, especially my Deafblind brethren, I hope you find yourselves reflected in these pages.

It is a truth universally unacknowledged that you could become disabled at any point in your life. No matter how perfectly your limbs, eyes, ears, and whatever else works, it could all change in an instant.

If you age past fifty? Spoiler alert: Your chances of becoming disabled just went up by 50 percent. And maybe you won't read it as a disability (because nondisabled society doesn't want to admit that if you need hearing aids at age sixty, you're still equally as disabled as a twenty-five-year-old who has them), but it is.

Nondisabled society has some weird rules about who is and isn't counted. There's a lot of language used that elides disability itself.

In the aforementioned example, it is "seniors" who need disability support. Seniors get canes and parking placards and hearing aids, even reading glasses and special shopping hours so they don't risk themselves during COVID-19—but they get them all without the pesky moniker of disability, because they aged into it. Nothing *happened* to them. In nondisabled society, something must have *happened* in order for you to qualify for disability status. The origin point of your disability is a plot point, which strangers will ask you to reveal on a semi-regular basis.

Similarly, children do not get called "disabled"; instead we call them "special needs."[12] The media often depicts small disabled children as cutely heroic, with organizations embarking on quests to make their lives worth living, politicians and parents legislating for their rights, and strangers cooing at their adaptive devices. Unlike "seniors" (elderly disabled people), once special needs children reach their intermediate form—disabled young adults—they suddenly metamorphose from adorable strivers to burdens on society. That transition hurts. All the support that nondisabled soci-

---

12　One of those terms that makes my skin crawl. There's lots of them, though.

ety had offered you as a child is snatched away on your eighteenth birthday, and the careful house of cards your family has built for you will vanish in an instant. Suddenly you need guardianship, you need to prove your worth, your wheelchair is no longer cute, and you can't get the fun style hearing aids anymore. Also, you have to *pay* for those hearing aids.

Media reflects this view. Disabled children are given screen time only for their adorable qualities (Tiny Tim; Micah Fowler's character, J.J., from *Speechless*), but once disabled characters get older, they have to check other boxes. Or, more likely, they aren't there at all.

I'm not going to do a lot of unpacking of old disability theory debates in this book. So here's a crash course in some basic disability theory, so that the rest of the book can do the work of memoir and media studies effectively. I hope you'll stick with me; I promise it gets more interesting after this.

This book uses identity-first language (IFL).[13] Unless the wording is literally more elegant to say [the person] with a disability, I will be using IFL only. Why do I use IFL? Because my disability is

---

13 Identity-first language is one modality of disability linguistics. With it, disabled people identify as just that: disabled. Blind woman, Deaf woman, wheelchair user are all other forms of IFL. The not quite opposite but alternate mode of language is person-first language. PFL was popularized primarily by parents of disabled people and emphasizes the personhood of the disabled individual. To me, that emphasis feels an awful lot like compensating for something.

a part of who I am. Without that disability, I'm legitimately unsure who I would be. I might drive a car, be a teacher or even a detective. I may have done all kinds of things that are off-limits to me because of my sight. My disability does define the borders of my life. That's not a bad thing; it just is.

And "disability" isn't a bad word. It's neutral. It carries neither a positive nor negative connotation within this text, and I hope that my readers will carry that concept forth into future conversations. Unlike "special needs," "handicapable," "handicapped," or "Dis/Abled," the word "disabled" is not trying to escape the reality of the human body. Those other terms are often used by people who would like to politely pretend that your body is not different from theirs. Often, nondisabled people who use this terminology think that it is polite to pretend that they do not see the disability, and as a result, they erase it from conversation entirely.

Other linguistic "quirks" that you might notice: D/deaf. There is a difference between big *D* and little *d* deaf culture. Much of it has to do with how steeped in Deaf culture you are—whether you use sign language, whether you rely on certain adaptive aids, how much time you spend in Deaf communities instead of hearing communities.

When I use the big *D* versus the little *d*, I'm cuing the audience in to the ways in which a D/deaf character lives their life (or how I do). You'll note that I also use Deafblind rather than deafblind. It's not an accident. I used to use a little *d*, but then 2020 happened. As I found myself needing to rely on ASL, my hearing aids, and whiteboards for communications with hearing people out in public, the visibility of my Deafness magnified. It didn't make any sense to align myself solely with hearing culture when my identity was shifting along with the hearing norms of the larger world.

But what kind of modality does that mean I operate out of when it comes to identifying disability as a theoretical model?[14] This book doesn't entirely subscribe to either the social model[15] or medical model.[16] I think both are useful ways of looking at

---

14 I have a master's in women's history from Sarah Lawrence College. Please forgive me when I talk in Academic.

15 Mike Oliver coined the term "the social model of disability" in the early 1980s, in which he identifies that the disability is not something wrong with a person but rather is created by society. It suggests that fixing or curing a disability is wrong, and that it is the fault of society's being unwilling to include disabled people that causes issues.

16 The medical model is just that, the way that we medicalize bodies. The framework for medicalizing a disabled body is actually not that much older than I am; it was created by the World Health Organization (WHO) in 1980. It establishes: *Impairment* equals a loss or abnormality of physical bodily structure or function, of logic-psychic origin, or physiological or anatomical origin. *Disability* equals any limitation or function loss deriving from impairment that prevents the performance of an activity in the time lapse considered normal for a human being. *Handicap* equals the disadvantaged condition deriving from impairment or disability limiting a person from performing a role considered normal in respect of age, sex, and social and cultural factors.

the world. There are ways in which my body absolutely disables me; things that it does that define the boundaries of my life. However, society is also a disabling force. If we had more public transit, if self-driving cars were a reality, if the job market weren't so hostile to disabled people, I'd probably struggle a lot less.

The other theory of disability that this book addresses is the Disabled Systems theory.[17] I suppose this is the one that I subscribe to the most, because it says that you are not born disabled but that, by both medicine and society, you are observed to be disabled. That seems to fit my own experiences best.

But shifting your understanding of disability does not merely come from acknowledging that disability is everywhere and that it can happen to anyone. It also does not come from merely understanding how disability exists in the world. The way that average nondisabled people consume media about disability matters, and the context of those disability memoirs matters, too.

A lot of these disability memoirs are about making nondisabled people feel inspired by a disabled person's life's journey. This is not that book. If you walk away inspired, I'll feel that I haven't done my job correctly. To quote Stella Young: "I am not

---

17 Dimitris Michailaki, "The Systems Theory Concept of Disability: One Is Not Born a Disabled Person, One Is Observed to Be One," *Disability & Society* 18, no. 2 (2003): 209–29, https://doi.org/10.1080/0968759032 000044184.

your inspiration."[18] I don't care to be. Don't go out and climb a mountain because you read about a Deafblind woman who climbed Arthur's Seat. Don't decide that because I was able to acquire a graduate degree, you, a nondisabled person are a failure for not having done so. First of all, that's a false equivalency, and second, that's not the purpose.

If you are inspired to do anything by this book, it should be the work of dismantling the ableist system we live in. It should inspire you to interrogate what you see in movies and what you read in books. It should, I hope, convince writers and directors and artists all over the world to think twice before they portray blind people in certain ways.

If I must be inspiring, then let it be the kind of inspiring that makes real change, not New Year's resolutions. Let it be the kind of inspiring that makes you want to call your congressperson and ask for updates to the Americans with Disabilities Act (ADA) that actually matter. Or to ask your favorite restaurant to offer large-print menus. Let it cause you to consider the ableism that lives within you.

It is difficult to write about disability without having to route around inspiration. Nondisabled society makes it so damned difficult for disabled people to do things, and forces us into solitude

---

18 Stella Young, "I'm Not Your Inspiration, Thank You Very Much," filmed April 2014 in Sydney, Australia, TED video, 9:03, https://www .ted.com/talks/stella_young_i_m_not_your_inspiration_thank_you _very_much?language=en.

so often, that it admittedly is remarkable when we are visible. My heart aches when I think about how different things could be if living a disabled life, visible in the public square, were no more remarkable than a white man walking down the street in a suit.

I wrote this book because I have lived a life of defiance, and I don't want other disabled women to have to be as defiant anymore. I want it to be less of a requirement that we be bold, that we be forward, that we welcome fear as normal. I want disabled women to live without worrying whether they'll be captured on camera and either lauded or criticized.

I wish that for myself, too.

Read on to shatter some stereotypes, for here there be dragons.

Helen Keller once said, "I would rather walk with a friend in the dark than walk alone in the light."[19]

As a community, we often use that quote to make it look like it's not too terrible to be blind. But at the core of that quote I see something that I don't like: I don't like the implication that blind people cannot be left alone. It makes it look like being alone is bad, that solitude is the worst thing that could happen to you. It supposes that blind people are meant to be helped.

The quote also enforces the blindness binary that I am so frus-

---

19 Joseph P. Lash, *Helen and Teacher: The Story of Helen Keller and Anne Sullivan Macy*. New York: Delacorte Press/Seymour Lawrence, 1980: 496–498.

trated by. Either you're alone in the light and therefore sighted or you're totally blind and you need help. That's not really how it works.

According to the Chicago Lighthouse (an organization dedicated to supporting blind individuals in living their lives independently) website, only 18 percent of people with "significant visual impairment"[20] have no light perception whatsoever. That's a very small number living in the darkness of which Helen Keller writes. Of the blind population, 80 percent, to some degree, is still sighted.

Blind people don't have language to describe their sight in nonvisual and nonmedical terms. We are given the language of the sighted, but it isn't enough. It's never enough. The best language that I've found in the world to make sense of the experience of sight is by using the language of photographers.[21]

We see with restricted views,[22] through pinholes,[23] with dead

---

20 "What Do People Who Are Blind See?," Chicago Lighthouse, January 28, 2016, https://chicagolighthouse.org/sandys-view/what-blind -people-see/.

21 In a book by a blind writer, which uses footnotes, yes we're also using photography metaphors.

22 A limited camera view angle, obscured by tools or the width of the lens. Similar to macular retinal degeneration or those with limited periphery.

23 A pinhole is a "photographic camera having a minute aperture and no lens," *Merriam-Webster's Dictionary*. Similar to macular retinal degeneration and retinitis pigmentosa.

angles,[24] without perspective,[25] on a Dutch angle;[26] some of us experience random motion.[27] There are a million different ways to be blind. I am halfway between two worlds, blind and sighted.

I'm out here, alone in the light.

Personally, I see with a single lens, which has restricted views and occasional motion disruptions. My lens blurs out at a distance; it's really only good for close-up work. If I'm lucky, the aperture[28] won't stick when I transition from light to dark. Usually,

---

24 A dead angle is "an angle outside of a fortification that cannot be reached by the direct fire of the defenders" (or, the view of a camera), *Merriam-Webster's Dictionary*. Similar to monocular vision much like mine.

25 For some blind people who have monocular vision, we lack depth perception.

26 Also known as a Dutch tilt, when the camera is tilted on its axis so that the world is slightly off-kilter. Some blind people's eyes can't focus the way that sighted people's can. Could be similar to those with severe nystagmus.

27 Random motion is when a camera is moved around while recording—often used in horror films. People with nystagmus and astigmatism will experience this.

28 Aperture is the part of a camera that controls the flow of light. For me, and for many other blind people, our eyes don't dilate the way that they should, thus mimicking the experience of a broken aperture, blowing out our shots (like a lens flare) until the flow of light is controlled.

the aperture sticks and I find myself standing like a deer in the headlights for a minute after a dark-to-light transition; sometimes I get lucky and for some reason I don't have a problem.

But to me, it isn't a lack of sight. I can't conceive of seeing with two eyes; heck, I don't really understand how sighted people see. The idea that you can see individual blades of grass or a bird on a faraway tree . . . it's just as strange to me as it is to you that I can't read a street sign.

Blindness can manifest differently not just from person to person, from condition to condition, from cause to cause, but from day to day.[29] It can shift based on the kind of light that you're in, what tools you use to read or to watch TV.

And yes, blind people do in fact watch TV. We consume media just like the nondisabled do, and let me tell you, I'm not happy about what I've seen: Every instance of blindness I have seen on television has been the same kind, the same fumbling lack of sight that begs for guidance, that relies upon others to keep them safe. The kind of blindness that nondisabled people assume is universal.

It is the kind of blindness that causes people to grab me by the arm, to insist that I must need help, that I can't cross the street alone.

This is frustrating enough for me as a passive consumer of

---

29 I have been reliably informed that this is true for sighted people also. Did the blue-and-gold dress meme blow your mind? Memes, friends. Memes prove this.

media. But there's a more pernicious problem: these depictions of blindness then drive the social constructs that further hem us in.

And because I'm also D/deaf, we have to talk about that, too. I have moderate to severe deafness in one ear (it verges to profound, but we're not quite there yet), moderate loss in the other. I wear two hearing aids.

As with blindness, there are rampant misconceptions about Deafness, too. Deaf characters are only ever depicted with Deaf accents,[30] relying solely on sign language, and typically in Deaf-only cultural environments. It's rare to see a Deaf character without a deep connection to Deaf culture.

In 1884, Alexander Graham Bell referred to Deaf culture as a "great calamity."[31] And so often, in the nondisabled world, I find that people assume that Deafness is a tragedy. Something to be avoided at all costs—and, of course, no Deaf people should marry, because *Deaf children might happen*.

My Deafness is the kind of Deafness that means I read lips, and when I take out the aids I cannot hear the dog snore across my

---

30 A somewhat problematic concept, but very real. I have one. It manifests in the way that I say the word "kitten" or "Scottish" and tends to get worse when I'm drunk. It's more obvious when I speak French than English, driven back in all likelihood by the study of Shakespeare that I undertook as an actor.

31 Alexander Graham Bell, *Upon the Formation of a Deaf Variety of the Human Race* (1884). Yes, Alexander Graham Bell was a fucking eugenicist.

bedroom or an alarm set at normal volume. I can hear someone in bed next to me, but only if their face is turned toward mine. I suppose the best metaphor for it is that, unless you have a mic, I'm sitting at the back of the auditorium even if you're right next to me.

But Deaf people don't need oral speech or nondisabled norms to form society. Deaf culture is real, vibrant, and important. It keeps sign language alive and vital.[32]

My two disabilities have something in common: they're both social, constructed by a society that assumes perfect sight and hearing is normal—and required for interaction. They reinforce the assumption that perfect sight and perfect hearing are normal and are required for interaction. These assumptions then hem us into roles we must play.[33]

Because disability is constructed socially,[34] people see these specific images (totally blind and incapable of sight or direction, totally Deaf and only signing) so often that they cannot imagine that there are people outside those binary states.

---

32 American Sign Language, British Sign Language, French Sign Language, Japanese Sign Language . . . there are so, so many. Not to mention home sign techniques that most Deaf kids develop on their own. More on that later. . . .

33 Judith Butler's *Gender Trouble* is responsible for much of my thinking around the concept of disability as performance.

34 I subscribe to the social model of disability and the medical model almost simultaneously. It's complicated. There is more in disability than can be imagined.

I was fairly open about the process of writing this book on my Twitter and Facebook pages, and as a result I gleaned some insight into how people see me. Many people exclaimed that they did not think of me as blind or Deaf, and expressed shock at my identity as a disabled woman. These were people who've had my acquaintance for—in some cases—literal decades.

It is a theme that I hear day in and day out, from strangers, from loved ones, from the people who fill my life from morning to night.

"I don't think of you as Deaf/blind/disabled."

When people say that, it has the opposite effect of what I assume they intend. In their minds, having a disabled body is a negative trait, and since mine does not seem "that bad" I can't be disabled. But to me, it feels like they're not seeing me at all.

When these conversations happen, they inevitably devolve into an argument, one in which I am expected to defend my identity and the literal realities of my physical body against how they have contextualized my body in the space of our relationship.

It becomes my job, in these conversations, to convince them that my identity is, in fact, accurate. I will have to argue, cajole, sometimes even fight them to retain ownership of my body and the identity that I am comfortable wearing.

Every time someone says, "I didn't know you're Deaf," or "I don't think you're blind," it tears a hole in my reality.

Why is it the business of the nondisabled to determine what it means to be blind, or the business of the hearing to determine what it is to be Deaf? Why are people who don't use wheelchairs policing the visual of a wheelchair user?

It's not only that the language of disability itself is designed by the nondisabled. If it were just that, maybe deaf and blind people could invent our own language . . . and, to an extent, we have. Cripple Punk and the language of crip pride is certainly important and valuable. But it's about far more than linguistics. Disabled people have their own languages. ASL, home sign, facilitated communication techniques, braille, and Moon . . . those are all disabled languages that can often only be spoken within a community because the nondisabled have chosen to colonize our bodies with the language of ability. In order to connect, we are expected to use the nondisabled language.

Nondisabled people are the ones defining disability as a whole. They decide what is possible to live with, and what gets discarded as useless.

It is evident in the ways we design buildings (think about the placement of the ramp at your place of business), in the students who are mainstreamed versus those placed in special education. It is evident in the ways that some manifestations of visible disabilities, like those of Paralympians, are seen as navigable (even laudable), while others (like mine) are often greeted with the exclamation of "Well, if I couldn't see/hear, I'd kill myself."

Ability is moderated not by disabled people but by the people who observe them.[35] Much like Laura Mulvey's concept of the male gaze in film, I think there is an abled gaze—a gaze that both

---

35 Rosemarie Garland-Thomson, *Staring: How We Look* (Oxford, UK: Oxford University Press, 2009), 79–96.

creates freaks out of disabled bodies and decides how to categorize them.

I assume that by now you've started rifling through your mental field guide to disabled bodies and have more or less settled on the idea that I'm not disabled enough to qualify for the identities I have, because I live somewhere between hearing and fully Deaf, between sighted and fully blind.

You've landed on that decision because you assume that I do not want to be seen as disabled. Because being disabled is not a compliment, it is a curse. At least, that's what you've been led to believe.

How nondisabled people define me isn't something I enjoy thinking about, though it happens on a near daily basis. The comparisons to relatives, the questions from total strangers on public transit, and the definitions both legal and social that carry me through my day. I used to call myself only blind. I knew there was a rubric for the identification of blindness, but the rubric was fungible. I could sort of wave my hand at it and dismiss it. Saying I was "just blind, a little bit" was easier. Why?

Because the minute that I say I'm Deafblind, we have a much narrower and more complicated rubric. A way for people to look at my body and to see all the ways in which it doesn't fit the definition they've been given.

Which is why, before we go any further, we're going to have to talk about Helen.

2.

We Need to Talk About Helen

Breaking Gibson's Mythology

I don't remember the first time someone compared me to Helen Keller. Suffice it to say that it's happened more times in my life than the word "Quidditch" appears in the Harry Potter series in total.

My first high school (I went to three) was not what one would call accessible.[1] Up three flights of concrete steps painted dove gray, each rounded edge blending visually with the next—it was a death trap, and without a white cane I'm surprised I never succumbed to their slippery edges while dashing up and down them with hundreds of other students in the old brownstone where it was housed.

Ninth graders weren't allowed to use the elevator, and even though I was a blind kid without a cane, I was still a freshman. No exceptions.

---

1 None of them were, really.

So at 7:30 a.m. I found myself dragging my very late butt up the stairs to English class, too-heavy backpack weighing me down every step of the way, and I crashed straight into Mrs. Eyre, who was waiting for me at the inside of her classroom door.

"Elsa, can I talk to you for a minute?" Her voice was calm, her eyes weren't full of concern—this wasn't an awkward "talk" about the quality of my mathematics work, or yet another admonishment about the fact that my handwriting was an impenetrable disaster.

And absolutely nothing about the fact that I was two minutes late, despite the fact that Mrs. Eyre was a stickler for timeliness.

"You know, I'd really like Spencer to read his essay aloud this morning."

My stomach churned. Spencer had a crush on me. He cornered me by my locker, always walked next to me when we went on class field trips even though I tried to avoid him, sat next to me in every single class we shared. If this had to do with Spencer, I didn't want any part of it. Especially not if Mrs. Eyre was talking to me about it.

Mrs. Eyre charged on, oblivious.

"So I'd like Spencer to read his essay aloud this morning, it was so good and well written. But I need your permission first, because he wrote it about you. Would you mind?"

Of course I would mind.

The essay assignment had been to write about someone who you admired, and why.

I can't remember who I wrote about. If I had to guess, it was probably Susan B. Anthony or, I don't know, maybe Tamora Pierce.

It wasn't an important essay to me.

But Spencer's essay sticks with me, twenty years later.

A thousand thoughts ran through my head at once when she asked for my permission:

Please, no, he has a crush on me.

Please, no, I am embarrassed.

Please, no, I don't know what he says about me.

Please. No.

But of course, what did I say? I was a rule-following, obedient kid. When a teacher asked me to do something, I always said yes, because that's what you were supposed to do.

As a grown disabled woman, I wish I could grab teenaged me by the shoulders and tell her that her consent matters. But instead, that day, I slunk into my seat in the front row (next to Spencer, of course) and prepared for the oncoming shame.

Mrs. Eyre introduced the piece, making sure the class knew it was with my permission, and Spencer stood up next to me and began to read:

"I admire Elsa because she's like Helen Keller."[2]

I don't remember much of the rest of the essay. It's buried behind a shame wall that I'd prefer not to knock down—though a

---

2 This is another example of the inspiration porn that I talked about in the introduction. It's a method of making all disabled people live a way for nondisabled people to feel like they need to do better.

part of me wishes that I had a copy. I remember he said things about me going to school by myself on the subway, about those awful stairs and how I bravely went up and down them by myself. I remember it was all the ordinary things that the other students did in their school day, and the only thing that made it a miracle (and yes, I use that word deliberately here) is that it was a Deaf-blind classmate who was doing them.

"I admire Elsa because she's like Helen Keller."

Well, let's get this straight out of the way: I'm definitely not.

But in that moment, at the age of fourteen, I had to wonder: How far would I have to go to be my own person? To find out, we need to understand Helen Keller's legacy.

But where do I start? Do I start with the legacy that sighted people have given her? The legacy that she built for herself? The legacy that blindness organizations have constructed for her? There are many ways to begin.

While I would dearly love to start with Helen herself, with the true story of her life rather than the ableist constructions that have been built up around her, it only makes sense to start with William Gibson.[3]

In 1959, Gibson's play *The Miracle Worker* premiered on Broadway. The script was based on Helen Keller's autobiography *The Story of My Life*, which was published in 1903. Because she wrote it when she was still in school, Keller's autobiography doesn't

---

3　For my science fiction readers, no. Not that William Gibson. The other one. The playwright.

cover some of the more important parts of her life—for example, her work as an activist, her part in founding the ACLU,[4] her world travel. It is not a book about Helen as an adult.

William Gibson picked up her autobiography and mythologized it. William Gibson took Helen's words (words that beautifully articulate what it is like to be Deafblind, words that demonstrate clearly to me that she was a thinking person who desired social interaction), and perverted them.

Gibson is almost solely responsible for the monolithic image that we have of Deafblindness in our media. Where Helen's autobiography articulates the experience of Deafblindness quite elegantly, Gibson reduces her to "a savage" and describes her as "feral."

In the fall of 2019, I was teaching at a university in New Jersey, picking up my morning chai before going to lecture, when I spotted a bright teal copy of *The Miracle Worker* on the free shelf below the barista bar. I grabbed it, my guide dog Astra trying to snuffle the pages as I picked it up to inspect the copy. It was an old version, not a copy I'd ever seen before. When I saw the cover copy my breath slowed. On the front of the 1973 edition it reads, "One of the most beautiful and terrifying dramas of our time—the inspiring story of Helen Keller!" next to an illustration that looks more at home on the cover of a horror script than a drama about disability. Anne Sul-

---

4 "What You Don't Know about Helen Keller," ACLU Montana, June 27, 2012, https://www.aclumontana.org/en/news/what-you-dont-know -about-helen-keller.

livan holds Helen in what can be best described as a chokehold, while Helen screams openmouthed.

The back cover is worse. "The Wild Animal" it reads in sans serif font—"Deaf, blind, and mute twelve-year-old Helen Keller was like a wild animal. Scared out of her wits but still murderously strong, she clawed and struggled against all who tried to help her. Half blind herself but blessed with fanatical dedication, Annie Sullivan began a titanic struggle to release the young girl from the terrifying prison of eternal darkness and silence."

This is the Helen Keller of William Gibson's imagination. This is the Helen Keller he created for the abled gaze. Words like "terrifying," "savage," and "animal" are applied to Helen throughout the script, leaning on similar language that has been applied to people of color for the last several centuries that we identify as racist. This language is also ableist.

William Gibson's work relies on the language of white supremacy to depict what is unacceptable about Helen Keller.

There are other inaccuracies in his depiction, of course. Firstly, Annie Sullivan arrived to start teaching Helen when she was six years old, not when she was twelve. Secondly, while Keller certainly described her blindness and Deafness as a lonely endeavor, she never says anything that remotely suggests a "terrifying prison."

Indeed, the person who best refutes Gibson's lies is the source of his story, Helen herself.

Did you know that Helen Keller created her own form of sign language to communicate with her family? I had no idea until I finally sat down to read her autobiography while researching for this book. It was devastating to discover that by spitefully ignoring Keller I had missed out on understanding a part of my own disability.

In her autobiography, she describes it in a fair amount of detail: "A shake of the head meant 'no' and a nod 'yes,' a pull meant 'come' and a push, 'go.'" Keller would imitate the acts of cutting slices of bread and buttering them to indicate she wanted toast. She would shiver and indicate cold to communicate that she wanted ice cream.[5] Most Deaf kids have home signs; they develop their own ways to get what they need. I have my own, too. My colleagues in the science fiction world who sign can get my attention, can communicate with me if they really need to. A lot of the signs we use aren't "real," but they're the ones I use, and that's why we use them together.

In Gibson's play, the audience is given no indication that Helen has ever tried to reach for her family or that she is working to communicate with the tools she has at her disposal. Helen Keller is a silent witness to her own experience, and in many ways, an unwilling participant in her own education. This myth decentralizes Helen as the protagonist of her own life.

In fact, in the stage play, Keller only speaks one word of dialogue: "water." In many film versions she doesn't even say that, merely grunts and shrieks. She's rendered mute, voiceless,[6] not even using the home signs that allowed her to communicate with her family.

---

5 Helen Keller, *The Story of My Life* (New York: Signet Classics, 2010), 4.

6 When I say voiceless, I mean in the metaphorical sense.

Keller at one point described her experience of Deafblindness as being lost at sea, and that's certainly how Gibson portrays her. But unlike the Keller of *The Miracle Worker*, she articulates beautifully within her own work that she was seeking moorage. She refers to the time before Anne Sullivan came to her as "before the soul dawn," saying that she had a mind and emotion but her inner life had no form. It *is* telling that throughout her descriptions of her life Before Anne Sullivan (BAS for short) she identifies as having no power of thought. This feels very much like the influence of nineteenth-century ableism, assuming that because she did not think in the ways that nondisabled people did, therefore she was not thinking at all. It's clear to me that she did think—and carefully— about how to communicate and achieve what she needed.

The only reason that Keller herself described her inner life as thoughtless BAS is because the dominant paradigm that surrounded her told her that was how it was. In chapter 5 of *The World I Live In*, she described how she had empathy for flowers and how she talked to her dog. These are not the inner workings of someone without thought or empathy but of someone who operates differently from the community standard. In other words, the way that Helen felt ultimately about her old life is steeped in ableist interpretations of disabled internal lives.

But Helen's myth persists, even with all the books, essays, and speeches that she gave, in part because she allowed it to be perpetuated. Abled society assumes she was nonverbal because that is the story most often told. We also assume that she was miserable BAS because she speaks so often of how she was lost until she was introduced to the concepts that sighted people rely upon, even as her same writings suggest a rich inner life.

It is the implied silence that I object to most. Deafblind women are depicted as having no voice, no connection. But as anyone who's known me for more than five minutes can tell you, I've never been silent a day in my life. Nor was she cut off from the beauty of the world. Keller described that she enjoyed music in *The World I Live In*, too, and the changes in voice and tone that she could catch through the hearing that she *did* have[7]—which also suggests the depiction of her as entirely Deaf is inaccurate. In the same book, she writes about all the ways in which her senses were adaptive tools. Helen loved the world she lived in, and she knew it well. By smell, touch, and yes, even hearing.

So the first legacy we have to deal with is the nature of the disability we share. Not all Deafblind people are nonverbal. Not all Deafblind people are completely blind, or completely Deaf. Not all Deafblind people use tactile sign like Helen did.

Even when we are nonoral communicators, even when we do not use our voices, we are still not silent. American Sign Language, British Sign Language, Pro-Tactile, all are forms of communication, forms of speech. There are so many iterations of sign language all over the world because Deaf people find ways to communicate wherever they are.

Since Helen Keller is the most famous Deafblind woman in his-

---

7 Helen Keller, *The World I Live In* (New York: New York Review Books, 2004), chapter 5.

tory, and because her presentation is so all-encompassing—and because William Gibson chose to portray her as feral, unruly, and savage,[8] there is little space for Deafblind women to be any different.

The white supremacist, colonialist language Gibson uses isn't the only issue here. There's also the perspective that everyone around Helen Keller was there to save her from her disability. The entire play is people *talking about* Helen without her being able to hear them or talk back. Her family is looking to tame her. Annie Sullivan clearly wants her to conform. Annie Sullivan was not her savior but her educator.

It's interesting because Sullivan herself was educated by Perkins School for the Blind, after growing up impoverished in an almshouse. Where Gibson, and indeed most reviewers, regard Sullivan as a fanatic, I see someone who is desperate to give Helen what she herself did not have: an education.

It's such a delicate balance, to address their relationship in a way that honors both the work they did together and Helen's desire to connect. William Gibson's script did not attempt to ride that balance at all. And because of the phenomenal success of his play, we've never had the opportunity to examine anything different.

But it is this need to connect and to communicate that resonates deeply with me. Helen wanted to connect with a world that kept her at arm's length. I know that distance well; it is the distance of wanting to hear what I cannot, see what I cannot. There are times when it is difficult to live in this body.

8　William Gibson, *The Miracle Worker* (New York: Scribner, 1988), 48.

Why was I not told? Why was this not part of the story that I was given as a child, that she found her way out of the isolation that was part and parcel of her experience?

There are moments when Helen describes her actions early on in her autobiography and we cringe, because they are the actions of an ill-behaved child. One of the most famous stories about Helen, the first scene of *The Miracle Worker*, is when she gets hold of some scissors and tries to cut the hair off a child whose mother was the family cook. The child's name was Martha Washington. The action is meant to demonstrate how feral she is perceived to be, as well as to instantly make his audience afraid of the Deafblind child holding a pair of scissors so close to another living being.

This is one of those things where we have to stop the narrative for a second and dig into the history. Helen Keller's family had a plantation. Helen was afforded every privilege on the planet, because disabled people can have privilege, even as they are marginalized.

More generally, nondisabled children cut their friend's hair, too. They cut the hair off their Barbie dolls (or at least I did), and they make mistakes. The only reason that this sequence is cast in a horror-movie light is because there is a Deafblind child in the picture.

Disabled children are still children.

Helen describes an incident in her childhood where she caught her apron on fire because she could not see the flame (obviously). This is one of those blind-person skills that we learn the hard way. You don't learn how hot fire is, how far you must be from it to not get burned, until your hands and hair have been singed a time or two. Fire is a weird visual for me: it moves; it wavers; it doesn't stay in one place. It looks far away even when it's close because of that motion.

So much of this is about context and storytelling. Keller retells all these stories about what a hell-raiser she was, and Gibson uses these stories as examples of how disability made her out of control. Of course, Gibson's legacy is used by others, too.

In 2012, Seattle saw a new version of *The Miracle Worker* come to life on the stage at the Intiman Theatre. Dan Savage had rewritten Gibson's classic show into a drag performance. Some context: I've known Dan since I was . . . tiny. He knew my parents. If he saw me on the street today he'd probably avoid me, because I haven't been uncritical of his treatment of disabled people—and this is why. In *Miracle!* Helen Stellar is a drag queen. She is still Deafblind. For the most part, the show was problematic in all the same ways that Gibson's script is, but there was a particular sight gag that made me so sick I had to stop watching.

To stop Helen from getting off the edge of the stage, they put an invisible-fence dog collar on her, and every time she approached the stage edge she would get shocked.

Since I had been a Deafblind child wandering the streets of Belltown in Seattle, playing in a café where Dan waited tables, watched by my community . . . the idea that he could think it was funny to put a Deafblind person in a shock collar hurt more deeply than I could have imagined.

Gibson's legacy is one steeped in harm. The play is written

about Helen. She's a problem to solve with whatever brutal means the able-bodied people around her can find.

This mimics the real world, where nondisabled people talk *about* disabled people rather than *to* them. Strangers will address my mother, my partner, my former spouse, my friends, long before they will willingly engage with me.

Helen isn't centered in her own story, and neither are most Deafblind women.

As I read Helen's autobiography, I saw myself in the pages. I saw myself in her terror when a thunderstorm broke over her as she climbed a tree. I see myself in her joy of knowledge, the freewheeling acquisition of language that allows her to connect with the world, to know it better. I saw myself there because they were shared experiences that I'd had as a Deafblind child. It was the first time in my life I had ever felt that kind of kinship with a memoirist.

As she opens chapter 6 of *The Story of My Life*, she says something that stops me in my tracks: "I had now the key to all language, and I was eager to learn to use it. Children who hear acquire language without any particular effort; the words that fall from others' lips they catch on the wing, as it were, delightedly, while the little deaf child must trap them by a slow and often painful process."[9]

Becoming a master of words, of language, was not easy for me. As it turned out, I had more in common with Helen than not. But the differences between us are still enough that they matter.

---

9 Keller, *Story of My Life*, chapter 6.

3.

Language Acquisition Through the Sound Barrier and Other Deafblind Mysteries

I t is difficult to learn braille as an adult, and even harder to learn sign language. Your hands have to rely on sensitivity, flexibility, and context as they never have before. How to tell the difference between a six-pip letter versus five? How to curl your fingertips into a *q* instead of an *r*? Or, even more challenging, how to teach your eyes to understand a visual language at the speed of those who have been using it for their whole lives?

Your fingertips have been dulled over decades of use, used to blunt force instead of sensitive consideration of the subtle differences in a texture. You have no idea how to find the world beneath them until you've tried.

I started with knitting, with feeling the difference between knit and purl, folding yarn under my fingers until they burned with the rawness of the stitches.

Then I moved onto the braille alphabet.

The process of learning often begins with the hands.[1] It is how we discover as children—hands in the dirt, the sand, the grass.

We learn through repetition, over and over, whether it be brushing the tips of my fingers over every elevator pad, every braille sign, every doorway (echoing the pass of my fingertips over a mezuzah when I enter my own home—my very own physical marker that I have returned once again) or by repeating Latin declensions or French verbs until they are a rote practice in the back of my mind. My brain connects to the French verb *avoir* before it ever reaches for the proper spot in an ASL window.

In braille, a single dot is an *a*, at the top left of the cell.

Two dots at the top of the left of the cell is *b*. . . .

So on, so forth, until the cells iterate, until your fingertips discover that the cells don't merely sit in steady columns but that they hop into diagonals and new combinations of the tiny pips that your fingers must learn to identify. I struggle to bend my fingers into words that don't have depth across a Zoom screen, aching for my tutor's hands to force my knuckles into the formal shapes that make a language. I struggle to recognize her own hand shapes, often feeling useless for hours after each lesson, my brain melting under the strain.

I learn these languages with the tang of bitterness at the back

---

1 It is not a constant. Nondisabled children do, blind children do. But there are children who don't, for reasons of not having hands with which to learn or being sensitive to textures and more.

of my throat; my frustration grows with each failure and setback. I watch other blind people read so swiftly, while my fingers stumble over the cells, my brain trying to make sense of a sensory experience it doesn't understand. I feel ill equipped, uneducated—not a feeling I'm accustomed to. I have always been a quick learner, except, ironically, in this crucial instance. It also angers me because I have been cut off from *my* culture. Yes, I know of my Swedish and Irish roots, but I was not given the Deaf culture that I should have known. I should be able to be comfortable in a room full of Deaf people, all signing to one another, comfortable in the silence. But because I was cut off from the Deaf culture that should have been mine, I feel lost, out of touch with the community. This is one of the problems with being raised by hearing parents in a hearing-dominant culture. You lose context, culture, community, and more.

And the language I *was* given causes so much harm that it's hard not to take it personally. The English language is perniciously ableist. We speak in metaphor that constantly puts down disabled bodies, with phrases like "turning a blind eye" and "it fell on deaf ears" falling from our lips so easily. People often tell me it's not that big of a deal. But, of course, if you've been listening to your language make you sound stupid, ignorant, and useless for your entire life, when you've made a profession out of the craft of language, you cannot help but find pain in the ways that language cuts you to the quick.

ASL has its own barbs. All languages do. But English is troublingly ableist.

While clawing for purchase in the English language, while teaching myself the craft of language, I had to do it through the painful process of reading in print. I spent years clutching magnifying glasses and pointing the brightest lights I could at pages of historical texts before my Kindle came along.

I feel it every time I fail to read something with ease: Why, why was I not taught braille as a child?

I remember someone from the Washington Talking Book & Braille Library coming to our elementary school classroom, bearing braille alphabet cards and a smile. But she never took me aside, never suggested that maybe I should be coming to the library to access the literature available to my fingertips.

Why didn't my parents educate me to be a better blind person? Were they afraid?

I have always known that I was raised to supersede my disabilities. My parents did not want a disabled child. That's what society tells parents: You don't want a disabled child. You want a child with ten fingers, ten toes, two eyes, two working ears. . . .

Helen Keller's parents did the same thing.

It's clear that they wanted her to be nondisabled, to conform to standards that she could not have possibly met. Of course, it was the nineteenth century; of course there was little in the way of disability justice, or of the idea that her disabilities were a thing to see as a part of her, rather than a thing that had to be mitigated.

But the fact that my parents seemed to have the same attitude tells me that very little changed between 1900 and 1985.

———————

I start learning braille when I am thirty-three. I am, for the first time in my life, in a building primarily filled with blind people. I've not spent much time in the company of other blind people before this—mostly at disability studies conferences—but now I'm at a guide dog school, learning how to work with a Labrador as my daily companion.

One night in the student lounge, after yet another round of Uno (which is one of the few games we have that has braille printed on it), it comes up that I don't know how to read braille, and one of my classmates pulls out a deck of playing cards, her hands swiftly setting up a braille "cell" with individual cards, playing three-card monte with language right before my very eye, two sleeping guide dogs lying on our feet. It is the first time that someone really teaches me braille.

"I can see why there were blind people working for the French Resistance," I say, delighted to discover that the language of my people feels like something codebreakers might relate to. I think of the very small exhibit at Les Invalides in Paris, where I learned about the blind men who passed messages in braille under the noses of the invading Nazis.

I felt, for a single moment in that museum, like there was something more to blind history than Helen Keller or Louis Braille's development of the very written language I am considering. Their stories are presented with the inspiring narrative that able-bodied viewers expect, and while these blind men in the Resistance certainly are inspiring, they were not inspiring for merely living their own lives.

This is not only about how a blind person navigates and intersects with sighted humanity. This is about using the ignorance of the sighted to truly stifle evil.

"Yeah, it takes a little while to get used to it," my classmate says before shuffling the cards away. A small pang of sadness fills my chest as she does so, but I know we have to go to bed soon. We both get up early with our dogs.

I take the cards back to my room that night, trying to re-create the magic, trying to unlock the secrets to a written language that my fingers still won't access.

Today, I can still only read the buttons on an elevator. Maybe that should be okay by now.

But I'm a woman who has never been satisfied.[2]

———

At some point, one of my failing senses will fall victim to my diagnosis. There's no predicting which one it will be. It could be my sight. More likely it's the hearing, since I'm already up to two hearing aids, and even then I often can't hear someone with their back turned.

So my hands must learn to speak for me sometime, even if they're not prepared.

———

2 Lin-Manuel Miranda, *Hamilton: An American Musical*, 2015, Atlantic Records, MP3.

I must rely on a dog, following his lead like we're dancing. Or a cane, now that he's retired, carrying a beat as I swish my cane along the pavement.

It's possible that Helen Keller and I will end up having more in common by the time I am fifty than we have had thus far.

In fact, our most important similarity isn't being Deafblind. Helen was an activist. A socialist. A writer. A woman who traveled and gathered knowledge and developed her own way of processing her world. I, too, am all of those things. (Yes, even a socialist.)

But I am not some of the other things that Helen Keller was. I do not touch faces to understand what people are saying.

And, let it be known, I am not a eugenicist.[3]

In 1915, Keller penned an article for the *New Republic* in which she argued, "It seems to me that the simplest, wisest thing to do would be to submit cases like that of the malformed idiot baby to a jury of expert physicians." She was responding to the Bollinger baby case of 1915. The Bollinger baby had been born with "physical abnormalities." John Bollinger was born with no left ear, a skin condition that made it appear as though he had no neck. According to multiple sources, it is likely that John Bollinger would have lived had he been given lifesaving surgery. But Dr. Harry Haiselden made the decision that a baby born with such severe

---

3 Anthony Horvath, "Helen Keller: Physicians Juries for Defective Babies, Article in the *New Republic*, 1915," December 18, 1915, http:// eugenics.us/helen-keller-physicians-juries-for-defective-babies -article-in-the-new-republic-1915/217.htm.

disabilities should not be made to live. In interviews, John's family agreed, saying that the "poor little one"[4] would be of little use to society or anyone else.

Haiselden made this determination based on perceptions of quality of life, which he convinced the parents of in order to allow the infant to die, thus enforcing the belief that certain kinds of disabled people are better off dead than alive as burdens on society. The concept of quality of life has been used to determine whether disabled people should be granted medical care in a variety of scenarios, from Terri Schiavo[5] to present-day COVID-19 ventilator rationing.

The Bollinger case was covered extensively in national media, and that's part of why Keller ended up weighing in on this particular medical case. Everyone did. Scholar Kim Nielsen points out the obvious contradiction, that Keller believed deaf and blind babies had lives worth living while those born with other disabilities did not.

This use of a hierarchy for disability is reflected in present-day society as much as it was back then, and I think it is anchored in eugenicist theory. Not only that, but it elides that while Keller may well have believed that deaf and blind people deserved support,

---

4 Mary Waller, "The Tragic Case of Baby Bollinger," Jane Addams Papers Project, July 18, 2018, https://janeaddams.ramapo.edu/2018/07/the-tragic-case-of-baby-bollinger/.

5 Much like the Schiavo case, the Bollinger case resulted in the public outcry reaching out to the hospital directly and making appeals for the patient's life.

Keller still carried a lot of internalized ableism from her upbringing, and given that she also slid into oralism, this isn't much of a surprise.

Keller's solution for the problem of what to do when profoundly disabled babies were born, and when medical intervention was needed, was to suggest literal death panels to decide whether a disabled infant should be allowed to live. Keller goes on to say: "A mental defective, on the other hand, is almost sure to be a potential criminal. The evidence before a jury of physicians considering the case of an idiot would be exact and scientific. Their findings would be free from the prejudice and inaccuracy of untrained observation. They would act only in cases of true idiocy, where there could be no hope of mental development." Her trust in the medical system, as well as her rampant ableism and racism, strongly point to early-twentieth-century white-lady morals.

Do you know what I fight for more strongly than any other cause? Health care. I believe that everyone deserves proper medical care, to be treated with dignity, and that the life of a disabled person is every bit as worth living as any other.

In this, Helen Keller and I have literally nothing in common.

She also cleaved closely to her Christian faith, arguing that it was God who made her blindness bearable, that God brought her Annie Sullivan as her savior.

This is part of why the comparisons between me and Keller are so problematic. Because while yes, we share a disability, we are both socialists, we are both writers and well-traveled women, we come at life from such radically different philosophical places, and our disabilities manifest in such different ways that we are not identical.

But abled society likes neat and tidy categories of disability. So here we are.

The fact is, I didn't have *any* role models like me. Helen Keller was the only one presented to me, but it wasn't as a woman who was a writer or an activist, it was as a child, tamed by ableism— who learned to conform to a world that wouldn't have her any other way.

Keller leaned into that legacy. She conformed. She was celebrated by heads of state simply for having *learned to speak English*. It wasn't because she cofounded the ACLU or because of her often transporting writing. It was because of her "remarkable" story, now handed down to schoolchildren across the globe.

What kind of message does it send to Deafblind women everywhere that we must not only carry forward her inspiration but also the toxic ableist philosophies that she agreed with?

Personally, I think abled society is quite aware of what it's teaching Deafblind women with this legacy. We are meant to be saints and paragons, not women who roll up their sleeves and get to work.

They want us to conform to a standard that makes *sense* to them. In order to be Deafblind according to the world at large, I must speak with my hands, not with my voice. I must be entirely unable to hear or see, and of course, I must rely on others in order to exist safely and comfortably.

So when I stride comfortably down a street, when I open my mouth and speak not just out loud, but eloquently in response to people who question my disability, when I look at someone in the eye and ask a question, I'm defying every single expectation the world has for me.

I think back to that classroom where Spencer read his essay, and I wonder what would have happened if, instead of blithely comparing me to someone with whom I have little in common, he had compared me to the woman that Helen Keller actually was. Would he have faced consequences for making a bad comparison?

What would have happened if the education that I had on Helen Keller was more complete, and if nondisabled educators rejected the legacy that they chose to uphold? The education of disabled children is not merely about the actual lessons our teachers bring into the classroom but the subtle ways we are influenced by what they choose to share. If Helen Keller is the only disabled person you learned about in school—and chances are, she is—you're bound to believe a whole truckload of lies about disability.

If you're disabled yourself, you absorbed those, too.

If I'd had access to Helen's autobiography earlier on in my life, if I had been encouraged to read *her* version of events—even tainted with the lens of nineteenth-century ableism—I think I would have learned a lot about how I exist in the world. What my body can do. Why I write metaphors a certain way, what happens when a texture makes me feel emotion. These things could have helped me to contextualize my reality.

The education of any child is about both text and subtext: what you learn in school, what you learn inside your body, what you learn from the society that raises you. And sadly, the education of a *Deafblind* child is often about how best to conform to the world.

4.

My Body and Other Histories

My mother dug up some old family videos of me from when I was very small during the summer of 2020. They'd been transferred to digital for preservation, and it was the first time I'd seen some of these images of my childhood from a nondisabled perspective. The lens—the gaze—was my mother's, or my physical therapist's. Not mine.

In the first video it is my first ballet recital. I had vague memories of the purple brocade costume with pink roses on it, of the fact that I had worn it onstage. It's such a fuzzy memory that I almost thought I'd made it up, but no. It was real. In the video I am surrounded by dozens of other children in ballet costumes, a ballerina of pastels if you will. I'm very quiet. I can see myself in the video, tracking my fellow dancers carefully as I go through the motions with determination. Backstage after I performed, my mom asks me if I liked dancing.

"Yeah . . . " I say in my small child voice, staring at the flower that someone had given me as a congratulatory gift for being on-stage. My focus is on the flower, not on the hubbub around me. To the nondisabled observer, I'm adorably quiet. To me, I'm over-whelmed. My sensory overload has given me too much, so I focus down to something I can touch, that doesn't move, that looks beautiful. I stare at the flower.

In the second video I am younger. Probably more like two. I wear dark glasses, and the people around me call me by my birth name (which I haven't used since back then). My physical thera-pist offers me textures to touch, asks me to stand up out of a chair. I am learning how to be inside of my body. And then they pull out the thing that, even to this day, fills me with a certain amount of unease.

A ball.

The physical therapist, and my mom, and whoever is behind the camera all encourage me to throw the ball to someone, to any-one.

And in each instance I carefully carry the ball to its intended recipient. I do not throw. I am as cautious with a flying object as I would be with a crystal vase. Because without depth perception I have never quite known how to throw things.

To the nondisabled eye, I was cute and polite. But to me, I saw how challenged I was by the world I was learning to inhabit. That's obvious in so many ways.

Apparently I never learned how to crawl. I mean, I did, a little. I've seen pictures. But the period of time between floppy baby and standing baby was a fraction of the time most people spend.[1]

This isn't a humblebrag. I'm not saying, "I learned how to crawl faster than the rest of you nondisabled fuckers."

No, to me, it's actually a confirmation that my body has always been a disabled body.

It makes sense to me. To crawl, your head has to be down, you can't see what's ahead of you. Your hands, your feet, they're occupied with the business of catching you if the worst should come to pass. It's not sustainable.

I never learned to crawl, and for the rest of my life I've been cautious. My mother came to my classrooms and told my classmates that they had to be aware of me; that they had to catch me if I fell. That I would always approach a shadow with caution—because shadows are my lifeline. They tell me if there's a step ahead.

My hands have always been crucial. They've been my safety mechanism ever since I could use them.

I'm not sure what it says about me that I never crawled, but what I know is I haven't ever been the type of person to live by half measures.

As I've begun to confront the history of my body in the process of writing this book, I have learned that it has essentially never been nondisabled. The remove I feel from my own medical history is almost eerie, as though I were researching someone else.

---

1 Since this is an important part of neurological development I wonder what that means. . . .

Before we can talk about how I have *lived* in my body, we need to talk about it as a context.

Bodies like mine have historically been put on display. They have been hawked for as little as a dime, used to draw crowds to the freak show, displayed as oddities in museums across the globe, and much, much worse.

We're still viewed through that lens today, but it manifests differently. Instead of being put forward on the bally—"Come see the one-eyed girl!"—I am merely an object for inspection on the subway, or the blind woman who comes to an elementary school classroom and submits (cheerfully) to the battery of questions that second graders have always wanted to ask.

My body is constantly on display. It is viewed by people who try to determine how blind I really am. It is viewed by people who will ask, "What happened to you?" and it is viewed by people who will tell me, "You're too young to be disabled." They tell me that I'm beautiful and it's too bad, because my eye changes that on a dime.

Let me tell you the history of my body, in the style of those old masters, the researchers who cataloged the oddities of the past.

I appear in the Mütter Museum's catalog. My occluded cataract lies behind glass, in a case, among other medically interesting eyes. The first time I visited the Mütter I remember delightedly shouting, "Oh look, I found me!" and then I felt the eyes of the crowd shift, from the case to my face, and back again. Silently confirming what I already knew. My eye was quite literally on display there.

So—where does the occluded cataract come from? At some point in the first trimester, when my mother carried me, she had a rash. She didn't know what it was—in fact, she barely knew she was pregnant yet. She brushed it off. Later, she would learn it was German measles—also known as rubella.

In adults, it's a mild disease. Most people never even know they've had it. A three-day rash, a high fever. Some tenderness in your joints. But if you're pregnant, it will attack the child you're carrying. According to the Mayo Clinic, 80 percent of fetuses exposed to rubella in utero develop congenital rubella syndrome (CRS).

I am part of that 80 percent.[2] But wait! There's more! Once I was born, we discovered a whole domino effect of symptoms from CRS which wreaked merry havoc on my tiny body.

Congenital rubella syndrome has the following conditions attached to it:

- Growth delays.[3]
- Cataracts.[4]

---

2 We will play with statistics in this memoir. The odds are almost never in my favor.

3 I've always been small. I weighed five pounds nine ounces at birth. My father was six feet tall, my mother is around five eleven. I am . . . maybe five two?

4 Bilateral cataracts were noted in my eyes at approximately three and a half to four weeks. I had surgery to remove them on both eyes. Secondary membranes were removed twice more from the right eye. At

- Deafness.[5]
- Congenital heart defects.[6]
- Defects in other organs.[7]
- Intellectual disabilities.[8]

That's not even the least of it. If you want to imagine my body's various conditions as evil fairy godmothers, we can add some gifts to the list. I don't plan on sending out thank-you cards to the people who didn't get their MMR shots and then went to an NYC gay bar in the 1980s.

---

present, the right eye remains occluded and hazy, a white blue color that is mine alone.

5 The first evidence of a hearing test for me was in 1996. I received hearing aids shortly thereafter. Purple ones that were clear so you could see the inner workings. Mild hearing loss in one ear (which has degenerated) and moderate to severe in the other.

6 I was born with a septal defect and mild pulmonic stenosis. A large patent ductus arteriosus was ligated at four months old, and I have had a stable heart since then. But the scar . . . it traces my shoulder blade on the left side. It curves around to the left side, leaving scar tissue cutting through my healthy tissue, and pulling everything to the left. It causes me severe pain.

7 None that we know of, but honestly CRS is weird and things could emerge later.

8 Whether the dyscalculia is merely a part of the blindness or the CRS we'll never know.

From the heart surgery scar I received the following gifts: chronic pain due to my scar pulling the muscles to the left side of my body, and thirty-five-year-old fascial tissue that doesn't really want to be anything but.

From my right eye and its multiple surgical interventions I received: ocular migraines, which mean I wear a scleral shell[9] over my right eye.

But there are complications that don't show up in the initial diagnosis that show up in my medical records. Mysterious little oddities that crop up at the most inconvenient times.

For example, my hips have been interested in dislocating since I was an infant. It just happens sometimes, entirely out of nowhere. And then I spend a week on a heating pad, wishing that I could walk.

The ocular migraines started in college. I couldn't look at bright lights. My head would go light and woozy; I would see sparkling lights and then have to spend days in darkness. For a long time, we didn't know why. It turned out that my blind eye—the occluded cataract—had some calcium deposits in the retina. Uncovered, without a lens, they caused pain. But even with surgical intervention for the calcium, I still had the migraines.

But the fact is, I haven't *just* been affected by CRS. My body has recorded other traumas.

---

9 A scleral shell is a neat piece of nineteenth-century ocular technology that works in the twenty-first. It is more or less a thick plastic content lens. They were originally made with handblown glass, which is some of the coolest medical tech I have ever heard of.

When I was eleven, I slammed my left-hand pinky in the hinge side of a door, shattering the growth plate and the first joint. The joint fused, and my pinky has never been the same.

On my right wrist is a scar—it's small—I tripped on a metal grated step and punctured my wrist.

Across my arms are small pockmarks, a constellation of mosquito bite and chicken pox scars.

On my lower left thigh there is a scar from . . . I don't even know what.

Beside my right eye there is a scar—you would think it was from an eye surgery, but it's actually from an ill-fated sword fight.[10] No, really.

Inside me there is Sjögren's syndrome (dry eyes, dry mouth, hands that ache from day to day). Post-traumatic stress disorder (the triggers from my first pandemic are constantly being pressed during my second[11]). A repetitive stress injury in my right shoulder from using a white cane for too long, too fast.

---

10 I've been sword-fighting off and on since I was nine years old. Fencing foil, saber, stage combat, broadsword, Zweihänder, dusack, katana. I love the feeling of a blade in my hand in a way that I cannot express.

11 In 1985 my father was diagnosed as HIV+. He would spend the first eight years of my life fighting a disease that killed dozens of members of our extended family community, and the disease called AIDS would eventually claim him, too. During the coronavirus pandemic of 2020 I have found the echoes of my pandemic childhood haunt me more and more.

And this doesn't even account for normal aging.[12] Which will also happen to my body, because disabled people do that, too. We age. We do not exist in perpetuity in our single disabled state.

My body is its own medical catalog. Documented in pages and pages of medical charts, in the observations of the medical students brought in to see the marvel of the CRS baby born long after the disease had a viable vaccine.

I have always been a part of the freak show, even when it wasn't running anymore.

In the musical *Side Show* (which I remember seeing in its original run on Broadway in 1997) conjoined-twin Violet sings during the second number in the show that she wants to be able to walk down the street without notice and without attracting attention, that she wants "to be like everyone else / So no one will point and stare." It was the first time that I would recognize, out in the world, what I felt in my bones—that all I wanted was to be seen the same way the other children were.

But it was not to be. Because on the street, on the dating scene, and everywhere else, I was the sideshow.

Now that you know what makes my body different from yours, let's talk about how I learned to use that body.

It wasn't easy. There were lots of stops and starts. When I was very small, I was in physical therapy—the video I described earlier

---

12 In 2017, I tore a ligament in my right foot. Then I tore that ligament again a year later. It seems to like doing that. I'm not sure it'll ever be the same again, and apparently this is what happens as you get older.

is an excellent example. My PTs had me handle different kinds of textures, learn to see the world through my hands, and to navigate carefully, long before I would ever deliberately teach myself to do things because they were hard.

I don't remember the first time I was put on skis. I've seen the photos of me in my bright red parka, blue hat, and white skiing helmet painted with rainbow stripes. I'm also wearing my hideously expensive glasses while facing down the flat expanse of a mountain, too tiny to know whether it was a good idea.

I do remember slipping on ballet shoes for the first time, skipping across a slick hardwood floor in a tutu. I do remember the first time my feet hit the roughness of a tatami mat at the dojo, learning how to fall gracefully in a gi.

I do remember the first time I buckled ballroom heels on my feet. I felt like I was teetering too far above the floor. Later, I'd find social dance was where I felt the most at home in my body, other than the water.

It took me a long time to understand how to live in my body. Physical education classes were for nondisabled children who wanted to play like nondisabled children do. Normal child activities were a little more fraught for me than the average small human.

Skiing, while fun, was dangerous and terrifying. Ballet, while a delight, spun out of control (quite literally), and without support I was doomed to spells of vertigo that took me out of the running for *The Nutcracker*. I needed something else; I needed a vector of control of my own body.

My first pair of three-and-a-half-inch tango heels were an impulse purchase. I'd been dancing Lindy Hop, and it was fun being thrown in the air, knowing that my dance partner waited solidly underneath. The partnership of social dance allowed me freedom. Rather than having to constantly look for where to step, in the arms of a good lead I had the option to close my eyes and *follow*—and the elegance of that, the ability to move fast, to step lightly and to feel feminine, had an instant power that I wouldn't fully understand until I was much older.

But three-and-a-half-inch heels?

I'd barely gotten myself out the door to prom in a pair of quarter-inch kitten heels, wobbling down our front steps. Anything other than a flat sole was intimidating.

But I had watched people tango, and there was something about the mental calculations involved that suited my desire for control. I wanted to know how to move through a room gracefully, and I knew the only way to learn it was to dive straight into a dance that would require me to walk backward in heels, to dialogue with my partner in the shift of an ankle or the twist of a hip.

There are ways of debating in dance that don't exist in speech, and I wanted to learn them. I sought elegance, poise. Swimming had given me grace in water, but I wanted more.

I craved the elegance of women who could get attention just by walking across a room, or the ability to be noticed for something other than awkwardness or a disability that people were curious about. I wanted to be more than an oddity, I wanted to own the spaces I lived in.

Learning what it felt like to spin across a slick hardwood dance floor helped me walk confidently across other slippery surfaces.

Learning how to fall on a dojo mat and how to take a punch showed me how to survive when my dance skills failed, or I missed a step on the New York City subway. Most of all, I learned that the only thing I could control—since I could not see well enough to know the fall was coming—was how to land gracefully enough.

It helped me to pass for nondisabled when I needed to, even if I never lifted my eyes from the ground ahead of me.

Of course, none of those skills mattered until I had a white cane in my hand.

———

I grasped the long stick in my right hand, trying to hold it like a fencing foil. The instructor wasn't amused. She corrected my grip and told me to start walking.

I was headed to Oxford University in two weeks, for a summer program. I was sixteen, blind and deaf, and I had never traveled alone. I was going to study Shakespearean acting and British history. I'd always dreamed of the spires of Oxford, and I couldn't quite believe I was about to go there. In fictional terms, I was ready for my Mary Russell summer.[13] It was 2002, and flying was still haunted by the recent events of September 11.

———

13 Mary Russell is the protagonist of Laurie R. King's Sherlock Holmes pastiche series. The first book, *The Beekeeper's Apprentice*, tracks Mary's first meeting with the great detective on the Sussex Downs and follows her to her studies at Oxford University. In addition to being disabled, I'm also a Sherlock Holmes nerd.

To be successful, I would need one crucial tool: a white cane.

My family had never really given me this kind of help before. They hadn't encouraged me to learn braille or sign language. They had gotten me hearing aids, but I think of hearing aids as an adaptation that gives hearing people more ease, whereas a white cane or ASL are tools that work with the disabled person's reality.

Learning how to use a white cane is a lot of trial and error. You can master the basic techniques fairly quickly, but it takes at least a few years to truly become competent. You will slam your cane tip into countless sidewalk cracks, jamming your arm and causing nerve pain. You will tangle your limbs in the cane during particularly nasty falls. You will whack the shins of total strangers, trying to learn how to distance yourself from others. You will learn.

You grasp your cane in your right hand, and point it down in a Pythagorean shape. Your foot will consistently fuck up the ninety-degree angle, but it's a part of the geometry of blindness. When at rest the cane should stand so that the elastic cable bounces off your shoulder.

In most movies and television shows featuring blind characters, it is the white cane that bothers me first. It is usually too short by several feet, and instead of elegantly scanning the ground as a blind person would, the sighted actors stab at it, gaining nothing. There is nothing to be learned by stabbing the asphalt repeatedly.[14] In *Scent of a Woman*, Al Pacino's cane is black;[15] he flails it in his right hand while grasping on to a young man for purchase with his left. He never actually uses the cane to get anywhere. In Netflix's *Daredevil*, Charlie Cox knows where to lean his cane to pick it up, but then he ditches multiple canes in various alleyways. It's a convenient prop to signal blindness to the audience, not a tool that the blind character's life actually depends upon.

Let's talk about the flailing—it's not calculated searching. I will sometimes gently reach a hand out into the void on my right side, when I know something will be there that I can't see (of course I also turn my head, but that's not something blind characters in movies do, either). They flail their arms out in the direction of where they *think* the world will attack them. Searching for walls with their outstretched hands, completely ignoring that there are tactics to find walls and doors that do not involve caricatures.

---

14 Sometimes it's worth stabbing if there's an empty space where no empty space should be, but it's not a tactic they teach you in class. It's one you learn after pitching face forward off a curb because the storm drain is missing.

15 There is a reason for the white cane being white, after all. Around the world the white cane with a red tip allows people to recognize blind people and be careful around us. Some companies, like Ambutech, make more fun-looking canes (I have one in purple and white) but the symbol is important, and a black cane won't reflect in the dark when a car is coming at you.

The blind characters in the movies do not move like I do with a cane.

They do not cut through crowds like Moses parting the Red Sea. They do not seamlessly tap their way down a flight of stairs on the subway with ease. They fumble, they are clumsy. And, of course, they cling to their sighted minders, making the cane irrelevant.

They are not the blind people I know. True, some blind people move slower than I do (I've been called a blind shark before), but all of us have a certain elegance and economy to our movements.

That first lesson in white cane use lasted all of twenty minutes.

I would not have another orientation and mobility session to teach me how to use my cane until I was in my midtwenties.

Using a cane probably looks easy to the uninformed outsider. Stick the cane out in front of you and swipe. Keep swiping until you hit something.

That's not really how it works.

A white cane is like the blip on a radar screen. Both devices scan. A white cane scans the ground out ahead of you, the constant scraping sound an ever-present reminder of your contact with the world. It clicks and thwacks on objects in your path, and you can use it to poke and investigate things that block your way.

But the cane is much more than a scanner.[16] It is the textural

---

16   Some people don't even use the constant contact method of cane use, preferring the two-touch method instead. Everyone finds what works best for them.

cues that really make the cane a useful tool. With it in hand, you can tell the difference between a slick floor and a broken sidewalk, between ice on the road and a puddle. That information is often the difference between a cracked skull and arriving at work safely.

I struggle with explaining the cane to sighted people, because for them, the world is drawn in sharp relief. There is no question of where they are headed, whether they will make it through a doorway or down a hallway without crashing into a wall, or tumbling down a flight of stairs.

Guide dogs are a completely different experience. As with white canes, guide dogs are not depicted properly in most media. They're also very rare. In the early seventies a crime show called *Longstreet* featured a white German shepherd named Pax as a guide dog. The CW's *In the Dark* features Murphy and her guide dog, Pretzel, an adorable golden retriever. In both instances, sighted actors are performing blindness. In both instances, the dog is a trained acting dog.

Not only does Pretzel not behave like a guide dog, but Murphy doesn't handle him like one. She doesn't protect him, tucking him out of the way during seated scenes, or even really follow him around. In fact, she barely brings him out, using her white cane during most of the show (for ease of filming, I suspect). It's an odd choice for a show with a protagonist whose parents founded a guide dog school in order to support their blind daughter.

With a guide dog, I feel like I'm social dancing. There is a pull in the harness that you follow, like a strong lead on a dance floor. I think it's part of what makes a guide dog work for me. I dart through crowds with my dog leading the way, go down steps with a subtle tilt of the harness. I can tell the difference between changes in the sidewalk because of where the dog is. The most valuable thing about working with a guide dog is the speed and efficiency with which I get from point A to point B.

But it isn't in my own adaptations alone that I have learned about disability. Rather, it's in my received knowledge of the world. Not from family, or even my teachers, but from society and media. From the things we all watch, read, and listen to.

I wasn't raised to be a proudly disabled woman. I grew up ashamed of the body I lived in. I often wished I had not been born with one clouded eye,[17] with a damaged heart, with ears that didn't fully function.

As a result, I spend a lot of time lying to sighted people. I was taught that it was polite to lie, to make them more comfortable. When a sighted person tells me to look at a bird, or at the shadow of the moon, I nod politely. I say, "Oh yes," and I don't contradict them. I have become an expert at lying for abled comfort, and it is exhausting. I've been trying to unlearn it. To say, "I'm sorry, I can't see that," instead of plastering a polite smile on my face to

---

17　This has certainly changed, now I'd rather not wear the painted scleral shell that covers my aqua cataract, I prefer to enhance it with accessories!

fake-enjoy the beauty of a pine cone. These moments are about appreciating a world that I do not belong to. But I am pressured to lie about my existence in that world because it is better to lie than to make them feel bad.

I wonder what it would have been like if the messages I constantly received hadn't been about how little I mattered. How much my body was not something to be proud of or to live in well. I grew up wanting to hide who I was. Stashing my new white cane wherever I could when I didn't need it. I fought the physicality of blindness tooth and nail, to the point where, before I had the dog, no one really noticed at all. My family would forget, my friends would never think on it. It was worth the work. For a while. People could almost accept that I wasn't disabled—to the point where now many people fight me on the acceptance of the term for myself.

Passing as nondisabled is such a weird thing to be able to do. For those unfamiliar with the concept of passing, we'll take a second.

Passing is used in a few vital contexts, and because of intersectionality, one can pass in one context but not in another. For people of color, the phrase tends to refer to the concept of passing as white. Being able to fold into the power structure of whiteness is not possible for everyone, and passing has a lot of consequences because of racism. Being caught is dangerous. In the LGBTQ+ community, passing means being able to fold into the expectations of heteronormativity. You can pass for straight, or for cis. You can pass for the gender to which you have transitioned. But you can't always seamlessly pass and survive safely at the same time. Many bisexual women like myself, who date men, find that they pass for straight—which can be troublesome, since no matter who you're dating, your sexuality doesn't magically change. In Eve Kosofsky Sedgwick's *Epistemology of the Closet*, she reinterprets the Torah story of Esther as a coming-out narrative—a story in which Esther outs herself as Jewish.

In all these cases, passing offers a degree of safety, but at the cost of authentic selfhood. And it's no different when it comes to disability. Yes, if you pass as nondisabled you certainly do get to avail yourself of nondisabled privilege—until you can't. Until you need the elevator, and they won't give it to you. Until you need help, and people interrogate you. This can be particularly true for Deaf people, who can still hear some, or for those with chronic or invisible disabilities.

In many ways, passing for nondisabled is an exercise in both comforting the nondisabled and in discomforting them all at once.

I learned that I needed to pass because of my mainstream education. But I also learned it was what was safest. Being subtly blind is safer than being obviously blind. I'll talk about this more in chapter 7, but it is important to understand: I have known for my entire life that I am a target.

———————

The first time that I realized I was Deaf, I was seven. I can picture the classroom where it happened. We were sitting at a faux wood hexagonal table doing a vocabulary test. My classmate would read me the words, and I would spell them out in my blocky child-like handwriting. We turned in our tests.

I failed. I knew all the words, and in fact, the words I *had* spelled were correct. It's just that I hadn't spelled the right words. They weren't even the Deaf child's worst nightmare: the homonym. They were simply words that sounded similar, conferring confusion.

That was when my father was still alive. As one of my caretakers, he struggled with my hearing loss as much as everyone else did, but unlike everyone else in my life, he left behind evidence.

When I was eighteen, my deceased father's papers finally came into my possession. Several boxes of documents: his writing, his journals, his personal letters. Everything he left behind for me to learn who he was, ten years after his death. While dredging through his poetry, I came across a line where he referenced that he knew I could hear him even when I chose not to.

My heart broke. Because he died before I got hearing aids in 1995. He died before I could possibly have been able to hear him. Of course the hearing aids of the 1990s were clunky, they were large and not entirely reliable. It was difficult to learn how to hear with them in, too. A process in relearning the art of hearing that I would continue into adulthood. But they helped me enter the world of the hearing—the world my father inhabited.

I think back to that vocabulary test—our first confirmation that I was unable to hear like everyone else—and I wonder what it would have been like if he'd lived long enough to communicate with me in the ways that I can now.

If his frustration would have become understanding. If he would have found me the resources to learn ASL, to develop my disabled skills. I know he understood that I was disabled, because he was, too.

My education has been full of clues that I was not like everyone else. Much of it was steeped in ableism. My father didn't know that he was engaging in ableist standards, or even what the word would mean to the healthy raising of a Deafblind child. My father only knew what tools the 1990s were willing to offer him, and they weren't enough to stave off the poison of ableism.

5.

How I Learned to Stop Worrying and Identify Ableism

A Lesson in Radiation Poisoning

Radiation poisoning is what happens to your body when you have been exposed to the entirely invisible, extremely dangerous force of nuclear fallout. Most people are exposed to it because they have survived a nuclear attack, or because they work in an environment that has experienced fallout. Some people have lived on properties with high radiation levels without even knowing it.

Because radiation is invisible, there's no way to protect yourself from it. You don't even know it's hurting you until one day, you find yourself with nausea, open wounds, fevers, and more.

Ableism is like radiation in a nuclear plant—it's a constant. Always there. A deadly and invisible force. If you don't have protection from it, it will destroy you from the inside out.

When you are born disabled—or even acquire a disability later on—you are instantly exposed to its toxic force. Because it is a part of our society. Most people don't even know what ableism is until they're fighting it. Until they hate their bodies because that's what they've been taught to do.

Much like treating radiation sickness, there isn't a cure for ableism. You can only decontaminate, limit exposure, and cure the wounds that it causes. You can't make the existing damage go away; it will be there forever.

I was born to nondisabled parents and grandparents. I was placed in mainstreamed classrooms, with no disabled classmates or role models for twelve years of primary and secondary education and fewer than five disabled classmates in my six years of tertiary education.

Until I was a grown adult, I had no concept of what it was like to lead a disabled life proudly. I had no concept of a disabled life as worth living—at least not without hiding and suppressing that disability, trying to mold myself to the nondisabled expectations applied to me.

Building an authentic disabled self is impossible when the world is irradiating you with self-loathing (without even realizing it). It's important to understand how it happens, if you want to truly understand disability in this world. And if you're nondisabled, trust me, you're being killed by the invisible force, too.

Ableism in the Home

When I was a little girl I did not think of myself as disabled. In fact, if you'd told me I was, I would have been confused. We didn't use terms like "blind" or "deaf" at home, despite the fact that I wore high-index glasses and a hearing aid. I was just Elsa.

This was unusual. A lot of people who are disabled at birth are quickly relegated into the world of "special needs,"[1] and they are treated as though their body, while unique, does not have categories that it can slide into. While at first, the concept of not having a label may seem helpful, it also threatens to rob you of the community you might otherwise have. I know many people who were *no-light-perception blind* (see, there's that fun enforcement of monoliths again) or had slightly less acuity than I do who went to blind camp. I have physically disabled friends who did Special Olympics and adaptive camps for physically disabled children.

Having disabled identities can be helpful, because it gives you common experience; you can learn from each other. Skills that even sighted teachers or trained specialists won't know, because they've never lived in a body like yours. Specialized knowledge is such a huge part of learning how to live with a disability, and I feel its loss profoundly, every day. It wasn't until I spent time around other blind people that I realized I needed a guide dog instead of a white cane when I lived in New York City or its adjacent areas, for example.

But I was the only child with my conditions that I knew; my

---

1 My needs are not special. A special need would be requiring a unicorn to appear at every book event I ever host. I have disabilities that require accommodation.

family didn't even think of me as disabled. While that may seem harmless, or even a good thing, it hurts.

It hurts because when I started to claim the word "disabled," when my aunt Mary[2] told me that I might want to try a white cane, she was the first person to tell me that I was blind. To validate the realities of my body. Until then, the entire practice of acknowledging my body was an art of mitigating reality, trying to pretend it wasn't there.

My family treated me like I was nondisabled because, even though I know they love me and want me to be who I am, society didn't. They wanted me to fit in as much as possible. Which I think is part of why they educated me the way that they did, to reject and hide disability at every possible avenue.

---

2 Named for Mary Ingalls, the blind character in *Little House on the Prairie*. She, too, lost her sight to a disease, though hers was degenerative and not scarlet fever. Prior to my aunt's wedding to my step-uncle, I remember hearing comments about whether she should wear her glasses in the wedding, whether she would be a good mother. I remember internalizing the discussions about her disabled body, and even though I was told I wasn't "blind like her," I actually was. It's a form of the "girls like us" dialogue, trying to separate the blind from the sighted, trying to claim blind privilege for those we love.

Ableism at School

I was mainstreamed in private school.[3] For those of you who don't know the language, that means I was put in a classroom with non-disabled children.

Being mainstreamed is, by and large, considered a good thing. You aren't "too disabled" to play with the other children. Your educational needs are not "too difficult" to accommodate for within the "regular" classroom. You are, by and large, considered "normal." This, like many other compliments given to disabled people who can pass for nondisabled, is actually harmful, rather than beneficial.

Being mainstreamed means that, for the bulk of your educational experience, you may be the only disabled child in the room.[4] Until college, I cannot remember there being another physically disabled student in my space. To be clear, I had three physically

---

3 My family was told by doctors that the best place for me was in a small classroom. Unfortunately, the Americans with Disabilities Act was both new—signed in July 1990—and not enforced in private schools. Until I dropped out of private high school in the tenth grade and went to public school starting in eleventh, I had little in the way of Individualized Education Programs (IEPs) or legal support. Perhaps putting me in a public school would have been better, perhaps it would have been worse. We'll never know.

4 An experience that iterated into my adulthood. I am now often the only disabled adult in a room full of colleagues. This speaks to the legacy of institutionalization, I feel.

disabled classmates between the beginning of college and the end of my master's. One Deaf classmate, one blind classmate, and one wheelchair-using classmate. I know some of my classmates in middle and high school had learning disabilities, but it isn't quite the same as needing an accommodation for not being able to see the whiteboard. Or worse, not being able to participate in games on the playground like the rest of your class.

When you're mainstreamed, there is immense pressure to conform. From early in my educational career, I was told that changing the rules for me wouldn't be fair to the other children.

Let me give you some examples:

Is it fair to the other children if I didn't play dodgeball because they targeted me, because I was afraid that they would break my glasses? My family fought for years to keep me out of the PE classes at school. My family fought for years to stop the abuse of dodgeball or the frustration of physical sports that were truly beyond my reach. But I was told constantly that my inability to participate made me a bad classmate.

Is it fair to the other students that I needed to take a different kind of math than geometry, because my brain literally didn't wrap itself around the concepts?

I have never been able to read a whiteboard, and yet I had to fake my way through all twelve years of mandatory school, plus another six in college and graduate school, but it wasn't fair to my classmates for me to receive notes from the professor.

What is the definition of fairness in an abled educational system?

The Education of a Blind Girl: Required Texts

The Giver by Lois Lowry

For disabled children, this book is terrifying. It asks the question of who should live in a society built on certain values, a society that kills weak infants and elderly persons. As a disabled child, I had nightmares after reading this book, wondering if the day would come that I would be seen as inferior. In Nazi Germany, this was called the T4 Program.

MESSAGE RECEIVED: Your life is valued as less than others. It is a true but terrifying lesson I wish I hadn't learned in the fourth grade.

Follow My Leader by James B. Garfield

The only book I read in elementary school that was about a blind kid. A boy who plays with fireworks loses his eyesight and gets a guide dog. But why was it always about boys who go blind, and never girls?

MESSAGE RECEIVED: Blind people are not like you.

Of Mice and Men by John Steinbeck

Discussion of this book was painful, because my classmates would often generalize, talking about not trusting disabled people. And most important, this book was the first time my classmates began to question whether disabled people could have sex.

MESSAGE RECEIVED: Disability is read as untrustworthy.

The Poisonwood Bible by Barbara Kingsolver

What wasn't problematic about this book? But most of all, I remember that a physical disability was used as a metaphor, a way to show imperfection, a way to emphasize difference. I remember raising this issue in the classroom and being told it wasn't important.

MESSAGE RECEIVED: You are not as good or beautiful as your nondisabled peers.

The Miracle Worker by William Gibson

See chapter 2.

MESSAGE RECEIVED: Deafblind people are unsociable and need to be taught how to conform.

The Secret Garden by Frances Hodgson Burnett

I both loved and hated this book. I loved that they had a secret place; I loved so much about the prose. But it made me unsettled and sad that I would likely have to hide away.

MESSAGE RECEIVED: Being disabled is terrible.

Flowers for Algernon by Daniel Keyes

As the only disabled child in my eighth-grade English classroom, when we read this book I felt like there was a giant beacon over my head. The question was asked of the class: If you were like Algernon, would you take a cure for your disability? Everyone said yes. I felt so much pressure to agree, to say that yes, I, too, didn't want to live in my own body.

MESSAGE RECEIVED: No one wants to be like you.

I don't know what messages my nondisabled classmates received from these books, because I wasn't in their heads. I do know that after reading *Flowers for Algernon*, there was a shift. My classmates stopped looking at me as "weird" and instead started processing me as "disabled."

But it wasn't only in literature classes where I was seen as other. There are two examples of what it is like to be the only disabled child in a school full of nondisabled children that are both painful and that demonstrate the "radiation" I am talking about.

PE class. No one I have ever met liked it. If you did like it, I am a little baffled, to be honest. Physical education requires you to play with the other children at the same level that they do, the same energy, the same style. I remember disliking tag on the elementary school playground because everyone would eventually figure out that if they snuck up on my right side, I wouldn't see them coming and they could tag me that way. But when I moved to New York City and started at a kindergarten-through-eighth school as the only new incoming student, things changed.

They had "yard." Yard was grade-specific recess time. As a class, we would vote on what physical activity we would participate in. I could no longer opt out of tag or play on the swings instead. I was not allowed to decide what the best activity was for me—the rest of the class did.

And my class really, really liked dodgeball.

I was an active kid. I did aikido and ballet; I swam competitively; I liked to Rollerblade and play street hockey with my friends. But I was not a kid who liked throwing balls or having them thrown at me. I can't imagine why. It might have something to do with the fact that I don't have depth perception.

Middle schoolers smell fear like sharks smell blood. They will notice that you are weak somehow, and they will go for that weakness. I was a smart child. I loved to read, to write; I loved to pretend. I was a theater kid from the moment I could set foot on a stage. But dodgeball was not in my skill set. That should have been fine. It was not.

Five days a week I had to endure having a hard red rubber ball thrown at my head.[5] Five days a week I would try to come up with an excuse for why I couldn't participate in the mandatory "fun."

---

5 It is no surprise that I have an aversion to flying objects to this day. I flinch. I do not like flinching.

Five days a week I was told that I was required to. That in order to be a good community member, I had to play along.

While outside in the yard, my classmates threw things at me, an easy target; things got bad inside the classroom, too. I had one classmate, Joffrey,[6] whose favorite game was to see how Deaf I really was.[7]

He would chew gum next to my head.

He would scream in my ear.

He would whisper obscene and mean things to see if I noticed.

I learned to keep my face still, not to react, not to let him see that he was physically hurting me. It was my first lesson in how to take abuse, one that would serve me far too well for the rest of my life.

I learned not to let them see that I was in duress. I was eleven.

But it's a double-edged sword, because if you don't respond, the abuse[8] can get worse. After all, they're looking for a reaction.

---

6 The prince in *Game of Thrones*, and one of the darlings of my school.

7 Without the assistance of external instruments used by professionals, it is very difficult to tell precisely how Deaf someone is. You would need to test their hearing in multiple environments, not just using the barometer of annoyance.

8 According to the WHO it is difficult to ascertain the exact levels of abuse and violence directed against disabled people because not enough research has been done. Based on community evidence, I'd say the prevalence is great, and the lack of research mostly comes down to a disinterest in the dominant social structure to investigate the harm done to disabled people.

This is how I learned to survive being an outcast.

I don't know a single disabled person who had a disabled childhood who did not experience bullying. I don't know anyone who wasn't trained to submit to this kind of abuse because it was safer than asking for help.

This is how we're trained to be quiet when ableism affects us.

But at eleven, I hadn't yet learned to avoid asking for help. (Remember, I still didn't think of myself as disabled.) I asked for help, and I'll tell you what it got me: institutional abuse.

See, once my mom got involved, once the school started to have to *do* something about me, they decided that the problem wasn't the culture of the classroom or the school. It wasn't the bullies' fault.

No. I was too weird. I wasn't a team player. I clearly didn't know how to navigate.

They made exceptions: they let me work with the music teacher, spend time in the library, instead of going to the yard. But they also told me I had to play basketball.

Again with the flying objects.[9]

Toward the end of that horrible school year—a school year where I felt dreadfully alone, and which almost made me hate

---

9 In the ninth grade, at the same school with Spencer, the gym teacher would scream "Can't you see?" at me when I consistently failed to hit the birdie while playing badminton. I don't know if I'd say this radicalized me, but I did walk out and refuse to go back again.

school, I remember being in the classroom with one of my teachers by myself. We were talking, and he said to me, "You know, you
just need to learn to hide who you are a little better."

I have never forgiven him.

———————

If you're wondering why we're spending so much time on ableism
in schools, it is because that's where, for the most part, you are
taught to hate yourself. Not only by the teachers or by the source
material,[10] but by your classmates, who will exploit your disabilities, and by the system itself, which is not built for you.

You will be sent to buildings that are unsafe, you will go on
field trips that are unsuitable, and every time that someone abuses
you (and until the eleventh grade, there will be many of them) you
just have to take it.

I could read you the litany of my oppressors of both genders,
but it would be simpler to say that I found few classmates I could
trust, and I clung to them fiercely.

But let me also explain why I dropped out of high school.

In the tenth grade, there was a racist incident in a classroom,
and the school decided we needed to have a conversation about
marginalization. The entire tenth grade was pulled into a social

———————

10 Though the fact that there is no acknowledgment of disabled students
having sex in health class, and there are no positive representations
of disability anywhere in my literature or historical texts is . . . telling.

justice seminar for a week, a special unit to help us understand issues of race, sexism, and homophobia. During that seminar, we had segments where white students couldn't talk, where we were segregated if we didn't do the reading, and where we could say whatever we wanted about different readings.

During research for this book, I found my initial vocabulary test for the course. It included words like "bisexual" and "racism," but there were a few things that were missing. One, notably, was any notion at all that disability was a marginalization. When I tried to speak up, I was often shouted down by my hearing classmates (and by that point I had stopped wearing my hearing aid altogether because of what Joffrey had done to me. Wearing it was too dangerous).

When I approached the faculty to ask if we could talk about disability—perhaps the first time that I raised my voice to speak about my particular experience of the world—I was told it wasn't important.

That is when I got radicalized. Because after months of being in detention because I couldn't do math (but was honor roll almost everywhere else) after years of being told I was too weird, I broke. I couldn't conform any longer.

I broke free.

Ableism in the Workplace

As a disabled person, getting a job is rather difficult. Disabled people are unemployed at twice the rate to nondisabled people in the United States.[11] If you're wondering why, it's partially that there are lots of jobs that disabled people cannot perform by the nature of how nondisabled people set up those jobs[12] and how job descriptions are written.[13] Many jobs require a driver's license, something I will never have and do not wish to acquire, even if it's rarely actually needed on the job.[14]

In my early twenties, I was studying to be a teacher. I abandoned that particular career path due to a significant amount of ableism in the certification process (though I didn't know the language for it then). One particular summer job I applied to (which shall remain nameless because I really don't feel like suing them, but if you remember sending this email, I hope you

---

11 "Persons with a Disability: Labor Force Characteristics—2020," Bureau of Labor Statistics (US Department of Labor), February 24, 2021, https://www.bls.gov/news.release/pdf/disabl.pdf.

12 You do not want to put me in an open-office plan with two hearing aids, a guide dog, and one working eye. It's just a bad idea.

13 David M. Perry, "How Academic Jobs Screen Out Disabled People," *Pacific Standard*, February 14, 2017, updated December 3, 2018, https://psmag.com/news/how-academic-jobs-screen-out-disabled-people.

14 Oh, just you wait until chapter 5. . . .

feel awful) said they weren't comfortable hiring me because of my vision when it came to being a playground monitor.

I have been a playground monitor before. The children know to come and get me. I watch like a hawk; I wander instead of sitting and waiting for something to happen. I push swings, and I make sure every child knows—if something happens and I don't see it, get a friend and come to me.

But adaptation is, of course, nothing in the face of "blind people shouldn't watch children."[15]

The most awkward part of any job interview for me is when the conversation inevitably turns to ask if I need accommodations. Of course I do. I need a number of them. But I don't want the fact that I need accommodations to kill my job opportunities.

The hardest part of this book is knowing that any future employer might see it, read about my disabilities, and decide before I get a say that I am unemployable.

There is a risk to being seen.

Ableism in the Streets

Home, school, work. Places where you know the people who are doing you harm. Those are places where the sideways comments or the direct ones will settle in your bones and make them brittle.

---

15 Chapter 12 will talk about children in more detail. But the short version is this: as a disabled woman I am expected to stay far away from other people's children, and I am expected to never have any of my own.

The places where wounds form. Lifelong wounds that take longer to heal than you could imagine.

But home and school are not the only places where ableism manifests in the world. In fact, home and school are only the beginning.

In order to write this chapter, I went and asked my Facebook friends (populated by a remarkable number of disabled people) what the most common, benign forms of ableism are in their lives. After 388 comments, I had some answers: elevators labeled with encouragements to use the stairs instead; invisible disabilities and chronic illnesses being disregarded because "you don't look sick"; lack of changing tables for adults; lack of accessible bathroom stalls; stairs (no ramp); linguistic terms like "lame," "deaf as a doornail," "blind faith"; the term "accessible" used to mean other things; requiring phone calls instead of emails; family and friends and doctors telling you that the illnesses are all in your head . . . The list goes on. One of the things that wasn't mentioned directly, but got sideways glances, was catcalling.

Disabled people experience catcalling with alarming frequency, but the street harassment we receive is often a little different from what nondisabled people get. I'd like to give you a few examples, because I think it matters to understand that when I talk about harassment, it is not just a random stranger telling me that my ass looks good in a specific wiggle skirt.

I was minding my own business on the 4 train, the express between my dear friend Agatha's[16] house and mine. It was late. My

---

16 Agatha Runcible, the wild partygoer of Evelyn Waugh's *Vile Bodies*.

white cane sat between my knees, the top handle folded down so it didn't smack people in the face. I was reading a book—back in the days before my Kindle fit in my purse—a battered paperback. I'd gotten this trip down to a science. Read my book from Franklin Avenue until Eighty-Sixth Street, then switch my reading glasses for my distance-vision glasses, put away my book. Hop off at 116th and walk home. It was easy. It was normal. It was what I was used to.

Which is how I didn't notice at first that at 1:00 a.m. on the 4 train someone was looming over me. Honestly, I can't remember what he looked like. I can remember his voice, low and quiet. He said quite clearly, in the silence of a nearly abandoned subway car, the tracks rattling away in the background:

"So do you like it with the lights on or off?"

———————

Another day in New York City. Another day walking by myself. A woman in floral and pastels approaches me. I think she's about to ask me for directions. Instead, she grabs my hands.

"Jesus loves you. He'll heal your sight if you accept him as your personal savior."

———————

I am standing at another street corner by myself, the bitter-cold wind sweeping down Columbus Drive in Jersey City. I'm waiting to cross a rather difficult intersection on my way to the PATH train. Suddenly, despite the light still being red, I feel someone's hand slip into my left. I glance and see a woman I've never met in my life.

Before I can shake her off, she's dragging me across the street, talking as though she's known me my whole life. Midway across the street I manage to free myself and ask her to please not touch me.

Right there, in the middle of a four-lane street, she screams that I'm an ungrateful bitch. That I should have let her help me.

I cross the street, afraid not merely of the cars but also of the woman who is chasing after me, telling me I need to be a nicer cripple.

In the street you must perform. Your body must conform to the disability society has assigned to you, and if you don't, you will be policed by society.

Because ableism says we all must look the same.

Ableism in Faith Spaces

One of the places where the Americans with Disabilities Act does not apply is in houses of worship. It is perfectly acceptable according to the law for a church to not have a ramp, for a synagogue to turn down your guide dog, for a mosque to not have an elevator.

As a cynic, I have to admit I've always wondered whether this is because of the theologies that mark us lesser in G-d's creation. Of course there are other theologies that say we are gifts from G-d, and that the disabled babies born to people of faith are special blessings, that we are never given more than we can handle.

Neither version has ever worked for me, theologically. But my personal views on faith are irrelevant to the ableist constructions around it.

During college, I took a course called Christian Diversity. My professor, a charming middle-aged nun, really wanted us to see the beauty of the different kinds of practice. I visited a Quaker meeting, a Greek Orthodox mass, a Pentecostal church. I went to a Presbyterian church and an Episcopal church. And one day a friend asked if I would come with him to his Calvary Baptist church. It was a large building, all wood beams and old stained glass, and the parishioners were primarily Black. They wore brightly colored hats and white gloves, and the ushers appeared at a certain point in the service, holding trays of personal communion packets.

My friend, a deacon, led me through the vestry after Sunday school. As we walked, I saw that people were tightly wound around a young man with what I believe was Down syndrome. I watched as they laid hands on him, trying to pray his disability away. They spotted my white cane and proceeded to lay hands on me, too, asking Jesus if I could have my sight granted back. They didn't know I was Deaf, too, or that my brain could be construed as broken. But they surely wanted me to see as they did.

A few weeks later, a classmate on my conservative Catholic campus told me that my blindness was a punishment for my parents' sins.[17]

It is no surprise to me, as the daughter of an AIDS victim whose

---

17 I had recently given a talk about my father's death from AIDS, so my classmate knew full well that my parents were gay.

own church would not support educating its parishioners in the use of condoms to save them from the disease that killed him, that these spaces are often filled with ableism. I feel it in the liturgies that ask for blindness to be cured, in the prayers that reference cripples and sick men and that do not acknowledge that a disabled body is also, for believers, a creation of G-d.[18]

In the morning liturgy for a Reform temple service, we thank G-d for the miracle of giving the blind the ability to see. Every Saturday that I attend morning services I choose to reinterpret that blessing. I interpret it as thanking G-d for the ability to adapt, for the gift of a white cane or a guide dog. Those things are not asking to remove my disability, but the blessing of adaptation.

Those thanks are not steeped in the ableism that I see everywhere. But the dominant theologies that I see want to fix disabled people with prayer and the grace of G-d.

Ableism on the Internet

"You're using a sighted Twitter client," the blind man on Twitter accuses me. I have no idea who he is; all I know is that every time I go viral, both abled people and my fellow Deaf and blind people come out to play. They ask how a blind person could possibly be on Twitter or the internet at all.

In one instance, when I was published by CNN, my right eye, of which I am quite proud, was called a "nightmare orb."

---

18 Or at least that's how my theology works.

Ableism is ubiquitous online. It is like breathing air. While the Americans with Disabilities Act exists, it was created long before the internet was something worth paying attention to. One of the ways in which blind people specifically encounter ableism online is through the lack of accessibility. Websites willfully ignoring any legibility guidelines in favor of pretty graphic design. This is one of the ways in which the ADA must change.

Ableism in the Self

Perhaps the worst place where ableism lives is in our own hearts.

When it comes for you from your family, your friends, from the media you consume, the online interactions you have, the schools that teach you and the strangers you meet, it is hard to resist it.

I remember longing for contacts, for glasses that had an index like everyone else's. I wished for hearing aids that were invisible, for a pupil in my right eye. I longed to drive, to not need a white cane, to not need to glance at my feet more often than the sky.

I longed to be normal.

Ableism made me wish that I were something other than who I was meant to be. Ultimately, that did damage to my heart.

When I was fifteen years old, I met my black dog.[19] I'd gone through a series of traumatic events, some worse than others, and after September 11, my brain started to drown itself.

I started to think that maybe I shouldn't live.

---

19 A long-standing mythical depiction of depression.

It was easy to think that. People online who found out that I was Deaf and blind would say they couldn't live like I did. They would say they'd kill themselves. When I complained to one on-line friend—after a close family friend's son committed suicide—she told me maybe I should die if I didn't want to be myself.

I'm pretty sure it was one of those horrible things that teen girls say to each other. I don't think she meant to suggest that I should actually commit suicide. But I thought about it. I stood over an overpass for a long time, staring down at the cars, thinking about whether it was worth it to live.

I had never met a disabled person like me. I had never been told that being disabled wasn't a bad thing. That it was worth fighting for myself. That the doctors who doubted my survival were wrong. That the people who thought I was smart and cute, but maybe not capable, had the story all wrong.

Disabled lives, in my world, were glanced at askance. They were not noted. They were given little quarter. Which meant that ultimately my life wasn't actually supported, either. It wasn't delib-erate. No one said to me, "Your disabled life won't matter." It was more that disabled lives weren't celebrated or given equal balance.

That absence is what will kill us. That absence is what nearly killed me. It is as important to see others like you as it is to be seen.

When we are told to disappear, we do. The ableism seeps in through those words and assumptions.

It poisons our hearts and infects our souls.

Just like radiation.

6.

Your Vision of
Blindness Is Impaired

The Monolith of Blindness in Media

The CW's *In the Dark* premiered in 2019 to a cacophony of outrage from the blind community, but the show was much more complex than it first appeared. Featuring a blind actress as the secondary blind character and a series of questionable life decisions by the lead, Murphy (played by a sighted actress, handling an untrained guide dog), it's one of the few good examples of a blind life lived fully (and dangerously). Murphy smokes, has questionable sex, dates, and swears. Murphy is not the blind angel most of the sighted world expects. She's not cute or precious, she's a little bit helpless, and she's stubborn as fuck. If I didn't dislike the show so much I might even identify with her a little bit.

She also has a very cute golden retriever named Pretzel. And in one otherwise unmemorable scene, Pretzel is doing something I'd never have allowed my guide dog to do. He's sitting up, snacking on pieces of pepperoni that Murphy takes off her slice and feeds to him.

As hard as contemporary shows are *trying*—and they are—their depictions of the blind experience still fall flat.

In May 2019, I was living just outside New York City. I'd discovered newfound freedom at the end of a leather harness, with a black Labrador leading the way. We went everywhere; I could meet up with friends and go do things much more frequently. If you ever want to really understand what tired is like, I challenge you to go around Manhattan minus one eye, with earplugs in your ears, using a white cane. It's exhausting.

I went to my favorite bar. I'd been going there for years. They even had a drink named after me at one point—a gin martini with sage and cucumber that I'm going to have to re-create. Because I'm never going back there again.

Here's why: My dog, Astra, led me straight into the bar, up the rattly tin wheelchair ramp, and into the darkness that only a speakeasy can provide. I was so ready for that cocktail. It had been a busy week. And we were stopped, my friend, my dog, and me, at the door.

"I'm sorry, but you can't bring that in here. We don't allow pets." The server said, a tone of thin apology in his voice.

"Actually, that's not legal," I said, trying to keep my voice bright and cheerful, friendly. "He's a guide dog and covered by the Americans with Disabilities Act." I could have cited chapter and verse of the law that keeps me an equal citizen in the eyes of the law, but instead, I tried for friendly.

I tried.

After fifteen minutes of arguing with the host, who insisted that we could stay "just this once" as a courtesy, I made a phone call and complained to the Better Business Bureau. I was in tears on the sidewalk. With a guide dog had come freedom, less exhaustion, lots of changes that were good for me.

But also a new kind of pain and discrimination.

Murphy doesn't get a service denial when she feeds her guide dog in a pizzeria. She doesn't have people constantly stopping to ask her if they can pet her dog. Sometimes people try to help her when she doesn't want help, but the systemic bureaucracy that plagues the average disabled woman doesn't often come to her doorstep.

This is important, because when the complexity of disability—and the discrimination that comes with it—is elided in our popular culture, it's no surprise that most people in the United States don't truly understand the real disabled experience.

Imagine if, instead of using a too-short white cane and easily traversing the courtrooms of Manhattan, Matt Murdock (Daredevil) actually had to deal with the fact that there isn't braille in the building because it is landmarked.

Imagine if, instead of being allowed to finish her scene with the Big Bad in her mystery show, Murphy actually got kicked out of the pizzeria and had to deal with the feelings of inequality that follow from a service denial.

Imagine if Oracle had to use the garbage elevator.[1]

---

1 In ABC's *Speechless*, the mother of the wheelchair-using lead, J.J., explains the game "garbage or person," which describes how most

The biggest mistake is that these shows and movies make disability look easy—like all a blind person needs is a cane or a dog, and the rest of the world is easily managed.

As though Deaf people always have the interpreter they need. Any inconvenience that *is* depicted on-screen is meant to drive tension—ableism as plot device, rather than the irradiating force that it is.

Ableism is everywhere, dictating the ways disabled people must adapt to the world.

Practically speaking, any disabled character in New York City is going to have a problem getting around—as they would in most major cities. But let's use Manhattan as an example. After all, it's home to Daredevil, home to Oracle . . . you get the idea.

New York City is often hailed as the most diverse and navigable city in the world—yet disabled people can barely navigate it. Despite having hundreds of subway stations, a twenty-four-hour system, and a massive ridership, only 25 percent of the NYC subway is accessible.[2]

I lived in the NYC environs for ten years; the map of Manhattan is seared into my brain. I have routes—to my favorite bars, to my favorite theaters, to my friends' apartments, to Penn Station.

---

wheelchair ramps are in the alley and are double use for getting garbage in and out of buildings.

2 s. e. smith, "New York City Is a Nightmare for Disabled People," VICE, July 17, 2018, https://www.vice.com/en/article/pawb7b/disabled-people -new-york-city-how-to-fix.

And you know what? The whole damn city is inaccessible. Yes, there are curb cuts, but try using a motorized wheelchair down a crowded sidewalk. Even the subway stations that *should* be wheelchair- or guide dog–friendly often aren't because the elevators are poorly maintained.

Escalators aren't safe for guide dogs, either, yet for some platforms in Penn Station—specifically those to access New Jersey Transit—there are no alternatives.

Those are just the infrastructure examples. I haven't even started talking about what happens when a woman with a white cane cuts through Times Square at speed, confusing businessmen and tourists alike, all of whom refuse to get out of your way because *What are you doing out of your house anyway?* . . . I digress. New York City is a mess. But because the world is focused on the nondisabled experience of New York City, we see it as a paragon for access.

All of this is because the world has been built with a focus on the abled body, a body that doesn't have to care about what particular form of public transit you take, a body that doesn't need to worry about whether there's an elevator.[3]

It is this absence of understanding that really feeds the dearth of disabled representation in our media. Because if even the disabled characters you see on-screen aren't actually *living disabled lives*, the representation doesn't work.

---

3   Until you have a stroller, and then nondisabled people care about elevators an awful lot.

If you don't have to ask for a braille or large-print menu, if you don't have your guide dog constantly assaulted, if you're not experiencing opposition to laws that make your life better, then what exactly does the disabled experience look like? Because that's a fantasy world, and it doesn't hold up under most of the world building I see in our media.

———————

Much like history is written by the victors, dominant social norms create the world we live in. If disability is something nondisabled people fear, it's because you've been taught to feel that way.

In the 1800s there was legislation called Ugly Laws.[4] Among them: that a disabled person could not be seen in public after dark, that we could not be seen on the street. That the state of our bodies was something the general public needed to be protected from.

Disabled people were jailed and fined for being out after dark, for being seen in public, and for begging if they were unable to find work. Many scholars identify the Industrial Revolution as the period that shaped the modern conception of disability,[5] and I agree. The Industrial Revolution, by transforming every aspect of society, suddenly required all bodies to function in the exact same

———————

4 Susan M. Schweik, *The Ugly Laws: Disability in Public* (New York: New York University Press, 2010).

5 Lennard J. Davis, *The Disability Studies Reader* (New York: Routledge, 1997).

way—and any divergence quickly marked you as useless.[6] After all, if you can't work, the capitalist system sees you as a burden rather than a member of society.

And once you've been labeled a burden, it's a very hard identity to shake.

It's one of the things that I find most interesting about the media's depiction of disabled people. While out here in the real world it is difficult to find a day job when there are thousands of barriers to education, to transit, and to other basic human needs, characters like Matt Murdock (of Marvel's *Daredevil*), Melody Bledsoe (from *Switched at Birth*), and Bonnie (from *Jericho*) don't have to fight for their access rights on-screen.[7] Bonnie lives in a tiny community where the only people who use ASL are the ones who are related to her. Matt Murdock has superpowers. Will Traynor, protagonist of the 2016 film *Me Before You*, is an excellent example here of what I like to call the movie cripple.

Will has buckets of money. His parents own a castle. He lives in an updated carriage house, has aides for days, can access just about anything he wants. In fact, the only real access barrier he experiences in the entire film is that his wheelchair gets stuck

---

6 We see this in *Downton Abbey*, when Mr. Bates is constantly questioned by the rest of the downstairs staff about whether he can perform his duties because he uses a cane.

7 *Switched at Birth* does address Deaf culture and Deaf rights, but it is often a plot device.

in the mud *at the racehorse track*. But Will doesn't think that his disabled life is worth living because he can't stand up and ogle a pretty girl in Paris.[8]

Whenever I watch contemporary shows[9] that include disability, I find myself thrown out of the plot because I don't see the realities. I don't see people asking for a large-print menu and being told it doesn't exist. I don't see broken elevators. And that's a problem. It reinforces ableism, because if you don't see the struggles that disabled people go through on a daily basis, you might walk away thinking that this is an easy world to live in.

The first time that I saw a character face a real-world disability trope was on ABC's *Speechless*, when J.J.'s mom, Maya, takes him to his new high school and learns that in order for him to enter, he will need to use the ramp behind the school. Which results in Maya asking everyone to play a disabled person's least favorite game: "Person or garbage?"

Because the ramp that J.J. will use to enter his school is the same ramp that the janitors use to take their garbage in and out of the building. Before you think, *Oh, but it's not always like that*, I can guarantee you that it nearly always is. The movie theater that I went to for five years in suburban New Jersey? Garbage elevator. Garbage hallway. Any time I went to see a movie I had to ask them

---

8 In the romance chapter (chapter 10), we'll talk about how this movie affected the romance genre.

9 Or even noncontemporary. There were lots of disabled people in historical settings yet we never see any of them.

to unlock the door, and they always forgot, leaving me in a hallway that smelled like rotting popcorn.

The hotel elevator at a professional conference, when I was using a wheelchair while figuring out the constraints of my chronic pain condition? A garbage elevator.

The few elevators across NYC that connect wheelchair users to the subway? Used as public bathrooms and garbage dispensaries. Disabled people are not given dignified spaces in public to access buildings or transit systems. When we do ask for access, we are often questioned as to our ability, rather than being treated like everyone else.

It's rare that we see disabled characters actually navigate these issues in media. Our heroes and heroines seamlessly walk down city streets, traverse moving escalators that are never temporarily stairs, are never refused service. Which is definitely not the reality. The only times when these struggles occur are for dramatic tension or for comedic relief.

Our world, our Western society at least, is not built for disabled people to exist in public. Which is why it's so damn hard for us to get around. Television, movies, and literature have created a fantasy world through stories about disability penned by nondisabled people. Characters never have to prove their disability in order to exist in public, but the reality is much more complex.

We've been banned from public settings, institutionalized when it is inconvenient for us to reside with our families, and outright removed from the public square when necessary. In nondisabled society a disabled body is meant to be seen onstage, or in a medical study; otherwise it is best hidden from view. It's why, to this day, it still feels like an act of defiance for a disabled person to live independently, even with the most sophisticated adaptive aids and tightly knit communities.

In *Blade Runner 2049*, the original *Blade Runner*, *The Matrix*, and so many other science fiction movies, even abled people use technology to better adapt their bodies. They have bionic arms, robot parts, what have you. As an audience we think, *Sure, why not robot parts? Cool!* But when we look at a disabled character with hearing aids or a prosthetic, leg they rarely have the same reaction.

Of course, a hearing aid and a robotic ear are damn near the same thing. Yet one inspires fear and discomfort, while the other is edgy and revolutionary.

Nondisabled people only want to see disability if it is inspiring or if it ascends the human form. It's why so often we see solutions for wheelchair users that include exoskeleton legs, or wheelchairs with treads that can climb stairs. The nondisabled narrative is that we need to make disabled people fit the nondisabled paradigm, rather than shifting the paradigm itself to include them.

It's why cochlear implants are so popular in media. *Switched at Birth* is one of the few television shows that handles them well—it shows that cochlears are an option for some people but also clearly explains why not everyone wants one. One Deaf father gets a cochlear while his son and ex-wife reject them, in one storyline. In demonstrating the variety of the D/deaf experience and the variety of options for D/deaf characters in how to navigate their

D/deafness in a hearing society, *Switched at Birth* accomplished what few television shows have been able to—provide a nondisabled viewership with a context for nuanced disability.

A cochlear implant is not the equivalent of hearing for nondisabled people; nor, for that matter, is a hearing aid. It is a different kind of hearing, which you have to learn how to use—and unlike with a hearing aid, the cochlear is a permanent change to your body. To install one, you must have a hole drilled into your skull and machines placed in your body. It's no joke.

Think about it this way: when nondisabled people design characters and settings, they're usually missing the larger context. By designing adaptive devices that never fail, or that "fix" instead of adapt, they create nondisabled characters in nondisabled worlds.

Which means, quite possibly, you've never actually seen a disabled character. You've seen nondisabled people attempting to create a facsimile of disability, through the lens of nondisabled people trying to write about it.

Most blind characters in film are portrayed by sighted actors. They do all sorts of things to appear blind that no real blind person does. My favorite of these is the blind stare.

I can't think of a single blind character in television or film, or even literature, who uses their eyes the way that I do. Instead, most of them are staring into space. There is an unblinking gaze, aimed over the shoulder of the person they are talking to. Actors who have played blind characters even talk about how hard it is for them to "school their faces"—that is, to look as though they have nothing to say.

It is this particular trope that I would like to call bullshit on. I make faces! Silly faces. Stunned faces. Happy faces. I smile. I laugh. My face is expressive—sometimes too much so. A friend refers to some of my facial expressions as Face Journeys. My eyes move. They twitch and follow, they make eye contact. Yes. Even the blind one. People have actually commented that I make good eye contact "for a blind person." It always amuses me. The expressionless blind person is yet another falsehood borne of the notion that all blindness is the same.

This problem presents itself with wheelchair users in movies too—no one ever gets up out of their chair to grab something off a shelf. No one transitions from wheelchair to crutches.

And Deaf characters? Deaf characters always sign. But there is a wide variety of Deafness, too, and the relationship to ASL will change depending on the culture that the character has grown up in.

It's also about access. In the United States particularly, access to aids is limited. A white cane is an out-of-pocket cost; a wheelchair is often not covered by insurance; hearing aids certainly aren't. When you see these characters in film using expensive adaptive aids, you have to wonder: How'd they pay for them? How does Daredevil afford to chuck his white canes in alleyways all the time?

I protect my hearing aids with my life; the same for my canes and my dog. I do not leave them behind because they are a part of my body, in a way that's difficult for nondisabled writers to imagine.

Disabled bodies are not like abled ones. They come with de-
tachable parts. Parts that matter intrinsically to their experience.

A wheelchair is not a burden or a trap. It is a tool for independence. A white cane is not easily put to the side, it is the tool for
independent and speedy travel. American Sign Language is not
easily acquired, but it is a language like any other. Braille signs
and ramps are not "nice to have," they are the difference between
entry and denial. Without these things, there are no disabled bodies in public.

And that is precisely why the media needs to place them front
and center.

7.

How I Learned to Drive, Play with Swords, and Other Things You Shouldn't Do at Home

S ookie Stackhouse is disabled. It's right there in the first chapter of the first book in Charlaine Harris's thirteen-book best-
selling urban fantasy series the Southern Vampire Mysteries. In
fact, Charlaine Harris's other series, about Harper Connelly, also
features a disabled character.

But it's Sookie whose story I'm interested in because her story
went on HBO—not once but soon to be twice. Sookie identifies as
disabled because of her telepathy—she acknowledges very early
on that it is disabling to be able to hear the thoughts of everyone around her, except for vampires and werewolves. Sookie's experience of the world very accurately mimics the experiences of
people with audio-processing disorders: she can't sort everything
out, struggles with distraction, and often is treated differently by
the nondisabled around her because of the way that she copes.

While Sookie's disability and her ownership of it is obvious in the books, it completely vanishes in the HBO adaptation. Sookie no longer is portrayed as disabled.

In fact, there's very little in the way of organic disability representation in popular culture. Most disabled characters are written *in order to showcase* a disability, or to be an after-school-special type. It's rare to find a disabled character who is disabled and just . . . living their own life, without it having to be *about* the disability. That's especially true of disabled women.

It's part of what makes the book Sookie special. Sookie has lovers and friends and a job—maybe not a big important job, but it's the kind of job a lot of disabled people need to take in order to live independently. She lives with family because she can't live by herself due to the financial burden. Sookie Stackhouse is, inadvertently, the most accurate depiction of a disabled woman that I have seen in recent media memory.

Of course, no one else sees her that way.

General depiction of disability in television and film is tricky. It relies on tropes and shorthand to get the audience on board. When I talk about how, in real life, there is no monolith for disability, I'm talking about the random nondisabled people in the street who are constantly assuming I'm not blind enough to be blind, but I'm also talking about television and media in general.

Look, tropes have existed for thousands of years. It's how Grimms' fairy tales and Greek and Roman myths work. We know she's evil because she's a stepmother; we know he's a hero because he has a perfectly chiseled chest. In Amanda Leduc's masterfully crafted book *Disfigured*, she examines the many ways in which fairy tales create a lot of the monoliths and stereotypes of disability.

They're further reinforced by modern-day fairy tales, which brings me to one subject where I make a lot of enemies.

Disney, that beloved behemoth, is the breeding ground for a lot of bad disability representation. In the late eighties and early nineties, a rush of new animated Disney features hit the screen. I was exactly the right age for them, and I remember watching *The Little Mermaid, The Lion King, The Hunchback of Notre Dame, The Great Mouse Detective, Beauty and the Beast, The Rescuers Down Under, The Muppet Christmas Carol* . . . all instantly conjure childhood for me.

They all, to one degree or another, deal with disability. Of course, *Hunchback* is the obvious and most problematic version, but it ties pretty closely with *The Great Mouse Detective, Beauty and the Beast*, and *The Muppet Christmas Carol* for Most Ableist Children's Movie, and certainly influenced the way I thought about myself. Like everyone else, I was indoctrinated into antidisability culture before I could even start to think about it.

When Disney+ debuted in 2020, I ran straight for my favorite childhood movie, featuring Basil of Baker Street. I'd grown up reading the Basil books and the Sherlock Holmes books. I'd watched the Jeremy Brett Sherlock and, of course, Disney's mousey version. (In fact, I think I killed my VHS copy.) But I stopped cold in the middle of the film when I discovered (because we all have faulty memories, and I can be forgiven for not catching blatant ableism when I was six years old) that the first villain in the story, the nasty bat kidnapper, is disabled. He has a peg leg, and it's used to effect in a number of different ways, each time making it clear that the disability is coded for how creepy and scary he is.

I can't quite get over it now. I can still coo over Toby, the delightful basset hound, and Olivia and her crumpets. But it aches to know that one of my favorite movies was already teaching me that my body was one that I should be ashamed of.

General disability representation is heavily reliant upon these tropes. And tropes can be useful—look at the tropes used in fan fiction, or the horror genre, for instance. There is only one bed,[1] or a creaking door to nowhere, instantly means something. But the meanings shift when they're applied to real people.

In 1997, Disney released the live-action version of *Mr. Magoo*. I'd always hated the cartoon, since it's essentially about mocking blind people for tripping, falling, and running into things. Disney's revival featured a statement saying that they didn't mean to offend blind and low-vision people, but I have to wonder . . . If you need that kind of disclaimer, why make the film at all? Comedic manipulation of blindness is yet another one of those tropes that I look at and find fault with.

---

1 Kristina Manente, "The 'One Bed' Trope Finds Popularity in Predictability. But Which Fanfic Pair Shared a Bed First?," *Syfy Wire*, March 25, 2021, https://www.syfy.com/syfywire/theres-only-one-bed-fanfiction-trope.

Media has power, and these tropes are more than just tropes. They are the building blocks of ableism. They teach audiences how to view disabled bodies—how to laugh at us, how to fear us, how to distrust us.

So what tropes am I referring to, exactly? I'm so glad you asked!

My background is in humanities scholarship. I'm a historian by training, a cultural critic by practice. My activism is fueled by the ability to look at the world and understand the social underpinnings that control it. And one of the ways assumptions about disability are enforced is by the way disability is performed in media.

So let's switch gears for a second to do some experiments. Instead of walking you through them in a dry academic way, though, I'm going to do something a little different. I'm going to do as many of them as I can.[2] I used TVTropes.org to source most of these, because honestly, where else? This is what the internet is for.

Blind People Driving Cars[3]

In . . . well . . . look at the footnote, okay? In everything, blind people drive cars. It's considered funny. Oh no! The blind person

---

2 Within reason, safety, and the certain knowledge that there's a pandemic on.

3 *Scent of a Woman* (1992), *In the Dark* (2019), *Come As You Are* (2020), *My Blind Brother* (2016), *Sneakers* (1992), *Percy Jackson: Sea of Monsters* (2013), *Spy Hard* (1996), *Blind Fury* (1989), and the TV series *Top Gear* and *MythBusters*.

who cannot see is behind the wheel of a car! How funny! I knew when I started writing this book I was going to have to drive a car.[4]

It was a hot, unusually sticky day in Seattle when I sat down in the driver's seat, for the first time since I was fifteen or sixteen years old. Eeyore had made the somewhat dubious choice to let me drive her car—ironically, in the parking lot across from the middle school I had attended decades before.

It wasn't my first time driving. My mom says she let me drive her giant boat of a BMW Mercedes taxi named Hitchcock, though I can't remember it at all. The driving lesson I do remember was with my Estonian step-grandfather, who had never quite lost his accent. He was gruff and sharp, all edges and exacting expectations. The first time I drove with him was on Mercer Island. I can still remember it. The sky was gray (when was it not in Seattle, after all?), and we were in the Mercer Island High School parking lot on a weekend when no one was there. I think it was fall. I sat in the driver's seat of his silver Volvo and gripped the steering wheel with terror as he growled at me about not running into imaginary cars.

When, close to my fifteenth birthday, I went with an ophthalmologist's note in hand to try to get my learner's permit, they let me take the written exam and then asked me to take the eye exam. Surprising no one, I failed miserably and was not granted a license. So while my friends accessed the freedom of the open

---

4 In a parking lot. And no, I am not telling you whose car I drove, but let's call her Eeyore. We prayed before I got into the driver's seat. No. Really.

road, I was stuck asking my mom, my friends, my grandparents for rides—or using the bus. But I adjusted.

Fast-forward nearly twenty years, and here I am behind the wheel.

I cannot see the rearview mirror; I cannot see either side mirror. I cannot read the speedometer or any of the other dials on the dash. At that point I almost bailed, thinking that perhaps it would be better if I told my readers this particular experiment was, in the end, unnecessary.

With Eeyore's direct instructions, I put the car into drive, and she tells me to gently push on the gas. I realize I'm holding my breath. Oh G-d. I'm *driving*. Who thought this was a good idea?[5]

Eeyore tells me to drive toward an orange blur she calls a cone. The car feels like it's moving too fast,[6] so I try to brake. Everything about how little I can see is in sharp relief.

I absolutely should not ever drive a car on the street. Nor do I want to. The physical sensation of driving was unsettling to me, the metal box I had control of outside of my periphery in a way that I have never experienced before.

Is it a trope that a blind person could theoretically perform? Sure. I drove a car. But a blind person voluntarily driving a car probably has a death wish, and unfortunately, most of these characters driving are *completely* blind.

---

5 Me. It was me. I take responsibility for my actions here.

6 Five miles per hour is not too fast. I was told I was allowed to go up to ten. I did not.

Blind Swordswoman/Weapon Master[7]

So remember how I refused to take PE classes after a while? Well, guess what I did instead? Stage combat.

See, sword fighting isn't actually a sport that requires sight (and yes, I know some sighted people out there are currently clutching their pearls and saying, "But you're playing with sharp objects!"). Because so much of sword fighting is about physical geometry, and the sensation of touch, I find it less difficult to love this trope.

The part that bothers me about it is when the sword fighting or weapons mastery seems to be a manifestation of super senses. While Chirrut Îmwe from *Rogue One* is portrayed as fully blind, he is still sword-fighting, stick fighting and shooting things with precision and ease. The film leans on the concept of the Force to get this across, but there's an underpinning of the fact that because he can't see, his focus is better than that of the sighted people around him.

In *Game of Thrones*, Arya Stark is briefly blinded via magical means in order to complete her training as a member of a guild of assassins. The blindness is a test of her skill. Once she's proved herself, her sight is returned.

These uses of the blind-swordsman or -swordswoman trope pin the sword-fighting ability on supernatural means, rather than on skill. That's where the issue of the trope lies.

---

7   *Game of Thrones*, *Rogue One* (2016), Zatoichi series.

Face Touching[8]

I want you to touch your face. Yes, I know we're not supposed to do that now that we're in a pandemic. So wash your hands first. Okay. Here. Close your eyes and lift your hands to your face—this part is really only going to work in an audiobook, but this is a multimedia experience—start with your forehead. Feel your hairline, then for your eyebrows. The gentle curve of your ocular sockets[9]—my right eye is sunken in a bit more than the left. I can tell the difference, but that's because this is a unique feature of my face.

My fingers will also brush against the hard case of my hearing aid, the soft fuzzy undercut that keeps my hair out of it, and a pair of thick glasses. Your face touching mileage varies depending on the accoutrements your subject wears.

Most people are relatively symmetrical. Feel the slope of the nose, the small dip between the nose and the lips.

Now imagine doing this to a total stranger.

I recoiled typing that, I hope you recoiled reading it. The idea that blind people touch faces in order to understand what people look like is very weird to me. I don't touch most people's faces, certainly not people I don't know. Yet the idea that blind people touch faces persists—probably because Helen Keller learned to lip-read and understand people by putting her hands

---

8 It's everywhere.

9 But don't poke yourself in the eye; that is not what I'm asking you to do here.

on their faces. It's how she learned to speak from Anne Sullivan, and how she communicated with people like Eleanor Roosevelt.[10] But once again, Helen isn't everyone.

It's just not done, friends.

Echolocation

So. This is . . . real. Daniel Kish, a blind man from California, developed a way to echolocate. He teaches other blind people how to do it—it's *real*. Which is super cool—but my big beef with this trope (and with Daniel's assertions) is that not all blind people can do it.

Specifically, Deafblind people can't really do it since it requires hearing.

But Daniel does. He clicks. It's real. Someone should write about it in a non-weird superpowery way. Much like sword-fighting, it's a skill, not a supernatural ability.

Blind Seer[11]

When I was very small, I could still see shadows through my now-blind eye. It was the final death throes of my rods and cones, showing me what little they could as the computer disconnected.

---

10   "A Rare Recording of Helen Keller, Anne Sullivan, and Polly Thompson." Accessed via the Seattle Public Library. (Union City, NJ: Listen & Live Audio, Inc., 2013).

11   *The Others* (2001).

For a long time, that meant that I saw shadows out of one eye. I suspect this is where some of this trope might come from—the idea that a blind person can see things that aren't really there, because they aren't. They're a part of the world that the sighted cannot access but that the blind can see. An in-between, which feels just outside the realm of the possible.

Token Twofer

If you really want to get pedantic about it, I'm a token fourfer since I'm Deaf, blind, queer, and Jewish. Five, if you add being a woman. The idea that people can't be more than one thing is a problem. It reduces marginalized identities down to single identities, rather than intersectional and fully articulated humans. People are allowed to be complicated. Disabled people are allowed to be more than disabled, they can be nerds, or queer, or any number of other identities. Yet our media consistently boils disability down to a single identity.

Blind Leading the Blind

At guide dog school, I was sometimes the most sighted person in a room.[12] I would be the one to tell my classmates that they should avoid a chair or tell them where to sit down. We would bang on chairs to tell people where there was an empty seat, and

---

12 Sometimes my vision changes depending on light or other context.

we would shout if we found an obstacle. Blind people can guide each other—that's not a joke.

Blind Without 'Em[13]

I think for non-glasses wearers, there's this idea that if you take off your glasses you can't see anything. I mean, I guess everything gets extra blurry for me, but it's not like an on/off switch. Yes, people who wear glasses can still see. We don't need to fumble inarticulately for the door.

Sliding glass doors, however, are my particular form of kryptonite, and I have been known to run into them at full speed, then slowly slide down them in a cartoonish fashion. Do not endorse this trope.

It also encourages people to think of blindness as an on/off switch. When people see that I wear glasses, they assume I'm not really blind—but glasses don't fully correct blindness, they simply give you a helping hand to see something in better focus.

Blind and the Beast[14]

In the *Fantastic Four and the Silver Surfer*, the Thing has a blind girlfriend whose name is Alicia Masters. There's this idea that

---

13 In TV when someone can't see anything without their glasses.

14 *The Shape of Water* (2018), the Thing in the Fantastic Four franchise.

blind people can love only ugly people. Or, that the only person who will love a monster is blind (or otherwise disabled; see the Oscar-winning film *The Shape of Water* for the context around muteness and this trope). This cuts both ways. It assumes that blind people don't ever experience visual attraction for their partners (I do, and so do other blind people with certain forms of blindness), but it also assumes that we have no ability to appreciate beauty at all. The other cut is that the perception of ugliness or monsterdom can only be overcome by someone who is unable to see.

Either way, it's a shitty trope that needs to be kicked to the curb.

Blind Date [15]

A blind woman walks into a bar. She sits down, introduces herself to the person she set up the date with.

It's a blind date.

Usually, this is played for laughs. A blind person shows up on a date, and the sighted person is surprised by their appearance,[16] because do blind people even go on dates?[17]

---

15 You're going to kill me with these. No, seriously. I hate it.

16 Kenneth in *30 Rock* goes on a blind date with a blind woman, and it does not go well. Mostly because Kenneth tries to be "helpful" and the writers play it for laughs.

17 We do!

Blind Musician

One of the ways in which blindness is often depicted as exceptional is when a blind person can play a musical instrument. This also happens with Deaf people. Ray Charles, Stevie Wonder, and Diane Schuur are all examples of real-life musicians who are blind. A lot of reality TV shows like *America's Got Talent* and *The Voice* go in for this trope, having judges and audiences simper over the fact that a blind or Deaf person has superseded their body in order to make art.

But believe it or not, blind and Deaf people can play the piano without it being inspirational. Full stop.

Blind Mistake[18]

Blind people making mistakes are often used for comedic effect when it relates to their lack of sight. But the difference between a knife and a fork is easily managed if you know how things feel, and most blind people are capable of information management on a high level. I don't accidentally stab myself in the hand, for example. This trope tends to rely on blind people being ignorant or careless, when in fact carelessness for blind people often results in injury. We try to avoid that.

---

18 This is a form of blind leading the blind.

Handicapped Badass

Not only are you disabled, and you've figured out how to manage it, you're actually what we term competence porn. You're so capable you're handicapable![19] The disabled badass is often well armed or frightening by way of some other means. Not quite a hero—usually an antihero, due to their disability—but they definitely fight crime.

The handicapped badass is probably one of those tropes I neatly fall into, as a Deafblind sword-fighter with a small but well-maintained lack of self-preservation. I often get told I seem like a fictional character, and I think this trope is why. I want to be a person, not a trope, without restriction on the hobbies I can or can't enjoy.

Cute Mute

Some disabilities get coded as adorable. Muteness is one of them. Elisa in *The Shape of Water* is almost childlike in some ways, her innocence preserved by the lack of oral speech (until she so precisely signs "fuck you" in finger spelling, and fucks a fish monster, whereupon that illusion gets shattered, thank you, Mr. Del Toro).

---

19 Typing this makes me want to vomit.

Disabled Alibi

Oh no, they couldn't possibly have committed a crime / stolen that precious artifact / hacked into the Pentagon . . . they're blind! Or Deaf! Or a wheelchair user! Regardless, the disability means that there's no way in hell the law is going to believe a disabled person did it. Disability as alibi is, unfortunately, wildly useful in real life.

Disabled Love Interest

Generally speaking, disabled people in TV and film who are romantic interests only stick around for a couple of episodes. They're there often to provide humor or shock value.

I have a shocking confession to make here.

I date. Yes, me. A Deafblind person. Here, I'll even prove it. In a couple of chapters you'll meet someone named Arthur.[20] He's made the dubious decision to date me, despite all the warnings on TV about blind people being choices you make only once. He says he hasn't watched nearly enough American television to get that message.

More on that later.

---

20 As in Dent, not Conan Doyle. He's a mild-mannered-looking cis dude from a distance, but then he opens his mouth and starts talking about crocodiles. I bet you think I'm making that up. I'm not.

Disabled Means Helpless

This one is not so funny. Unfortunately, everyone does think we're helpless victims. Often this comes hand in hand with the real-life experiences of being traumatized. See chapter 9 for more.

Glass Eye

In movies, glass eyes pop out of sockets, roll around on the floor, and generally are used for comedic effect or horror effect. In reality, glass eyes are very cool and also things you shouldn't take out of your head unless you have washed your hands. Of course, I may not always take my own advice, because glass eyes left in champagne flutes are hilarious and unsettle sighted people.

Hiding the Handicap

I mean, disabled people do feel the need to hide their disabilities with some frequency. I'm often told I should wear the prosthetic shell that matches my left eye rather than allowing people to see my occluded cataract. Disabled women especially are told to try and conform to nondisabled beauty standards rather than experience disabled joy in their own way. This trope is a pernicious and systemic enforcement of nondisabled norms. Cut it the fuck out.

Prophet Eyes

Cataracts are often used to signal spookiness. Either ghost-seeing eyes, or eyes that can see the future, but somehow otherworldly. This is part of why small children on the street have been known to point and shriek "Witch," because more often than not, the only cataracts they've ever seen have been in the eyes of scary creatures that came from some animated television show.

Deaf Composer

Everyone knows who Beethoven was. Yes, he was Deaf; no, we don't actually need to mythologize Deaf composers as magical.

Reading Lips

Generally, I'm fine with lip-reading in media—many Deaf people do it, even subconsciously. However, lip-reading is not what you think it is, directly reading words off someone's mouth. It's a delicate balance of context cues, facial expressions, and the stray words you catch that allow your brain to fill in the blanks. Lip-reading is not something that you can pick up in a few weeks, despite what literature and television would have you think.

Senses Compensate for Other Senses

No. My sense of smell, touch, and taste are not better because I'm Deafblind. I just pay attention to different things than you do. Moving on.

Deaf Enjoy Music

Very loudly!

This list of tropes isn't exhaustive; I could go another fifteen pages, and you'd be bored to death. But you get the idea. These tropes empower nondisabled audiences to feel like they know what's happening, even when the truth is far more complex than it looks, which—consciously or otherwise—gives the audience permission to look no deeper. But real disabilities don't exist without a person behind them, and that personhood is what's so often missing from popular shows and films. There are so many assumptions about who disabled people are, or can be; so many conditions in place before the role is even written.

So what's to be done about them? Where do we find them? Well, each trope tends to correspond to a certain genre. And perhaps unsurprisingly, the most difficult genre to be disabled in is horror.

But before we can touch on individual genres, there's something important to consider: why is it that I keep wanting to talk about blind and deaf *women*? Well. Because disability doesn't live in an oubliette, and the performance of disability is intrinsically linked to our performance of gender.

8.

Yes, Virginia,
Even Blind Men Can Be Assholes

The Intersection of Disability and Gender

Before I get too far into this chapter, I need to make something really clear: The gender binary is a lie. Nonbinary blind and deaf readers of this book may find themselves wondering where they fit in this particular bit of theory. When I talk about men and women in this chapter, it is specifically with regard to the ways that people assigned female at birth and people assigned male at birth have been socialized. Terms like "socialized female" and "socialized male" should absolutely be used here. If you're blind or deaf and socialized female, you may have a lot of the same experiences that I have, whereas if you're socialized male, your experiences may map better onto identified-as-male examples.

It is also important to acknowledge that there are trans, nonbinary, and two-spirit disabled people in this world, and their experiences matter, too. We need those stories and those experiences to be honored and shown to the world.

I have a complex relationship with my gender. As a preteen and college student, I often wore button-down shirts and slacks, peacoats and blazers. I found myself asking to be Sherlock Holmes for Halloween more often than the princess du jour. In high school, I toyed with gender expression, playing with binders and considering my gender more fluidly than I had before.

I was raised in the queer community, and I'd never been forced into any particular gender expression (except by my grandmother), so it didn't really occur to me that I might not be entirely gender-conforming.

But for me, there is complexity in gender performance. Once I saw that my disability made it very easy for people to not think of me as feminine, or as a woman, I started to push back.

I often wonder if, in the absence of ableism, I would be nonbinary, if I would find myself more comfortable without application of gender binaries at all. But I find myself uncomfortable with being they/them, when so often it ends up feeling like a removal of my whole personhood rather than respect for my identity.

I hope that other disabled people who identify as nonbinary don't feel that way. But for me, the inextricable erasure of disabled people's personhood runs so deep that I can't unsee it.

I am probably not going to make any new friends with this chapter, either.

Stephen Kuusisto opens his memoir of blindness, *Have Dog, Will Travel*, by describing a trip that he took to Italy as a young academic with some colleagues. He describes how he and his friends rented Vespas and drove along the coast. Steve rode behind his friend in a red jacket, hoping not to lose sight of him. While I love that this memoir of blindness requires a sighted reader to understand that blindness exists along a spectrum, I had . . . opinions about the context.

When I read that sequence, I knew I had to write this book, because as a blind woman—or more precisely, as a blind person socialized female—I would never have done that. I've done some stupid things, I've committed some acts of bravado, but I have been taught, for better or worse, that I am fragile, and that I must protect myself at all costs.

These differences in socialization are important because they ultimately create disparities that play out not just in media but also on the street. While blind and Deaf people who present as female are often victimized, those who present male experience other challenges. There is harassment across the spectrum.

In the Netflix *Daredevil* series, Matt Murdock's best friend, Foggy Nelson, calls him out on something very specific: he accuses Matt of using his blindness to get close to women and to touch their faces. Face-touching is such a pervasive myth that it's played for laughs here, but there's a much more frustrating layer: Foggy assumes that Matt will get laid.

The first major difference between blind men and blind women in film is that while blind women are assumed to be virginal, disabled men are assumed to be anything but. Will Traynor from *Me Before You* talks about how much he wants to flirt with a pretty girl in Paris as one of his reasons for committing suicide; Frank Slade (*Scent of a Woman*) visits a sex worker, though he appears to only do so to smell her hair. Murdock is a love interest and considered attractive, while women are frequently told that they're pretty "for blind girls" or shown to take little care in their appearance. *Switched at Birth*'s Emmett and Garrett both talk about having had sex and are considered hot. Emmett even has a motorcycle.

Blind and Deaf men are not subjected to the same value judgments placed on women's bodies, which absolutely bleeds out to other things. That's not just because of the way in which society treats gender but also because of the way in which gender and ability intersect. Women are allowed—even expected—to be frail, whereas men are expected to present in non-broken ways.

Men who can be both disabled and masculine are few and far between, at least in the public imagination. Veterans and Paralympians come to mind. We valorize disability when it is within the context of military service. It's one of the few acceptable ways to be disabled, because in the United States (and some other countries), the sacrifice of ability for your country is seen as a remarkable act.

I find that, mostly, it is cis men who enforce the gender binary when it comes to ability. If I had to make an educated guess, it is because they have been told by able-bodied society it is not *masculine* to be disabled.

In the mid-aughts, I wrote an essay about my experience at New York City Comic Con. I had been overwhelmed by how big the show was, and I found myself relying on my friend Audre for guidance, in addition to my white cane. As we turned down the center aisle, I spotted something. At first I was excited. A man in a suit carrying a white cane—perhaps a fellow blind attendee! I was filled with disappointment seconds later when I realized it was a character prop—he was dressed as Matt Murdock, Daredevil's by-day lawyer incarnation. As that registered, I realized something else—I had been struggling to get people to notice my own cane on the floor, and this might be why.

Nondisabled people using adaptive aids as props is dangerous. That was the thesis of my essay. Seems reasonable, right? Seemed reasonable to me. Still does.

For some reason, that argument was a flash in a pan. The blind men of Twitter came for me, talking about how *they* had never felt unsafe at a convention, and how they didn't experience the harassment that I detailed. Well. They were six feet tall and white. In my experience, the blind men I know don't experience the same kind of harassment that I do.

Deafness is different. Because, in a hearing world, there is so much toxic hearing culture, Deaf men do experience some of the same forms of harassment that Deaf women do. I think this is partly because, while we have a lot of enforcement of sighted culture, it is even more important in America that people be able to *speak*—and in the language that the audience prefers.

Toxic masculinity does not escape disabled men.

Racism does not escape white disabled people.

Homophobia does not escape straight disabled people.

Disability is not a get-away-from-all-toxic-stereotypes card, and I see that most in the men of the community, especially in the stories they tell and how they talk about their disabilities in public. Though white women in the disabled community are hardly exempt from being complicit in racism. Where women tend to write about their experiences as defined by the ableist system, often steeped in patriarchy, men write . . . adventures.

Blind man summits Everest, blind man comes up with a way to never use an adaptive aid and uses echolocation instead, blind man trains his own guide dog because no one will give him one to go on long dangerous hikes by himself.

I'm all for destroying expectations; hell, I do it myself. But I also believe in admitting that not everyone can do what I do—that I will not hold others up to the expectations that I have for my own body. Yes, I sword-fight (and have for many years), but I don't expect other blind people to do so. I do exclaim in sheer delight when I find others who do, of course, but that's not the same as "any blind person can climb Everest."

Where blind men are praised for these acts of extreme bravery, blind women are encouraged to sit things out. It's no accident that defiance is a core quality of female heroines in every genre, because women are constantly told that they can't or shouldn't. The blind men of our world are constantly talking about how they did things we would have been discouraged from doing.

While I think it's important to push boundaries (obviously), the act of pushing simply because you've been told you can't feels suffused in the toxic culture of masculinity. Why are all these blind men writing about how great they are out in the world, what brave nonsense they committed in the course of their blind lives? Because disabled men are often treated as lesser men, as not equal to the nondisabled men of their generations.

At the 2020 Republican National Convention, North Carolina Representative Madison Cawthorn pulled a stunt that disabled Twitter instantly condemned as vile: he stood up from his wheelchair on national television. Why? "You can kneel before God and you can stand for the flag."

Cawthorn is an extreme example, but he falls into the category of disabled men who fight hard against their own self-interest in order to demonstrate their manliness. Cawthorn's stunt falls squarely into the category of expectations for disabled men. They must push themselves further in order to prove that their masculinity outweighs their disability. Stand up when they probably shouldn't, walk when sitting would be better, climb dangerous mountains when maybe a smaller peak would be safer.

I'm not saying, by the way, that I think blind people shouldn't do the incredible, the ostentatious, the unimagined. We should. We should be allowed to surmount new heights and do new things regardless of whether or not it fits the picture of what a blind or deaf person should do.

The fact is, gender shouldn't matter, but because it's so inextricably threaded through our society like barbed wire, we have to acknowledge it.

In fact, even the narrative around caretakers of disabled people changes when it comes to men because they so often demonstrate their feelings about their disabilities through rage, which is often pointed at their caretakers.

In 2019, I published a piece called "How to Make a Paper Crane,"[1] about my experience with anger as a disabled woman; how I was told it was unbecoming to be rageful. How I needed to package my anger in ways that made people less uncomfortable.

But disabled men are allowed to feel rage on-screen. In the 1967 movie *Wait Until Dark*, Susy, a recently blinded woman, is terrorized by thieves in her own home. Regardless of Audrey Hepburn's less-than-stellar performance, there is one moment that really nails what it's like to be a blind woman in society.

Susy talks about being at blind school, about having trouble finding things, and then she says to her husband: "Do I have to be the world champion blind lady?" and he *says yes*.

While disabled men are able to fuck around and give themselves concussions both on-screen and in the real world, women must present the least challenging model of disability possible. They must be perfect, never making mistakes that risk either their social status nor their safety.

In *The Intouchables* and *The Upside*, two films about the same rich white man with quadriplegia, we yet again see how a carefree caretaker with no experience[2] can enhance the life of a disabled

---

1 Alice Wong, *Disability Visibility: First Person Stories for the 21st Century*. New York: Vintage, 2020.

2 As in *Me Before You*.

person. The difference is, that in this case, the protagonists don't fall in love with their carers. In both films, the caretaker is a Black man desperate to get paid, who has never done caretaker work for a disabled person before.

These caretakers are responsible for showing the disabled people that there is more to the world than moping in bed (or their expensive power chairs that no one can afford). These male characters go skydiving to feel nondisabled again. They race in fast cars; they go on expensive island vacations. They have massive parties and bask in near-nondisabled glee.

Meanwhile, disabled women are attacked in the streets and trapped in their own homes with criminals.

Disabled men are given the extreme privilege of living. They live dangerously, they live adventurously. They live.

Or they are the monsters.

Like in *Don't Breathe*, where the blind man is the monster. He is a rapist—though his rapes are committed with a turkey baster instead of a penis.

It fascinates me that these tropes fall across gender lines, but it makes sense. Society likes to sort categories. We like to understand where someone falls within the proscribed and accepted space that has been allotted to us. It's impossible when we start to bleed out from inside those boxes, like painting watercolors inside fine-line black outlines.

I feel for disabled men a lot. They are supposed to both follow the norms of their disabilities and force their way through them at key moments. They are expected to be manly yet celibate. Any reference to their sexuality on-screen is played for laughs—or horror, as in *Scream* and *Don't Breathe*. The idea that they won't have sex is what ultimately makes them monstrous. That they will be rejected is a reason to go on a killing spree.

While women are given the role of victim, disabled men are given the role of monster, or hero, at equal cost to their humanity.

One of the most haunting real-life examples of this is Oscar Pistorius. The world loved the man who popularized cheetah feet,[3] his Paralympic history a feat that few nondisabled people could imagine. But as it turned out, despite all the heartwarming memes, he was also a murderer.

The pedestals that we create for disabled men, the feats of strength that we thrill over, the stories that we create around them—it's the same cult of toxic masculinity that traps nondisabled men. And toxic masculinity, at its very worst, can kill.

Gender performance is tricky, and yes, it is a performance. We all make deliberate choices around gender presentation.

As disabled women, we hear a lot about being beautiful in *spite* of our disabilities. I find myself having to fight the urge to demur any time someone tells me that I am beautiful. I will glance

---

3 The style of prosthetic foot which allows Pistorius to run at the speed that he does.

aside, not make eye contact. It's not because I don't want to be told these things, of course, but because I have already been told over and over again by society that not only am I not beautiful,[4] I am actively undesirable.

Those doubts and questions followed me for a long time. There were always caveats: *You'd be so beautiful without your cataract, without your hearing aids, without the scar that runs across your back. You'd be stunning* if. *You'd be desirable* if.

Sure, beauty is in the eye of the beholder. But what if the beholder believes that you are asymmetrical? What if the beholder believes that your eyes twitch too much or that the scar that curves across your back is a distraction? What if your hearing aids and your glasses are ugly instead of a part of you? How long do you let the beholder tell you what you are?

Around the same time I got my first prosthetic eye, I also started hanging out with a costume designer—I've mentioned Agatha before. Before that point I had sort of not quite known how to

---

4 In 2010, I had to get my first prosthetic eye. In order to get it, I had to go see an ocular plastic surgeon. As he looked at my eyes, measured, and prodded, he talked to me about how he could make me better. "All we have to do is get you contacts, a nice painted shell, and you won't even look like you're blind anymore! You'd be so pretty!" He then went on to offer me free Botox, to take away the lines where I squint. I walked out of his office with a pit in my stomach. To this day, I only wear my painted shell when it is necessary. My whirlpool cataract is my eye, and I'll be damned if I hide any longer.

dress myself. I ached to get a sense of who I was through clothing and fashion—and perhaps start to feel beautiful.

Agatha helped me find dresses that showed off my legs, that gave me a sense of femininity, as well as a sort of armor. The ability to say, "Fuck the beholder, I look like I walked off the set of a 1940s movie."

These days, when I look in the mirror, I don't see the awkward blind girl who wondered if anyone would take a second glance. These days I glance in the mirror and see someone who flaunts her floral dresses like armor against a world that wants her to still feel small.

For me, and marginalized women of many intersections,[5] a pretty dress and some lipstick is an act of defiance.

Wearing a gown and a tiara, accessorizing my cataract until what you see from the back seats of the auditorium at the Hugo Awards is a sparkling moonstone in my right eye—that's a riot.

Aesthetic is an act of protest.

Because society wants to keep me confined in a box. That box is labeled "cute."[6]

---

5 Disabled women, fat women, women of color, women who dress modestly for religious reasons . . . the list goes on.

6 Keah Brown's #DisabledAndCute was wonderful—it opened up a whole world of conversation for disabled people to talk online about finding themselves attractive. But it is still a word with . . . implications. Cute. Not "beautiful." Not "stunning." Not grown-up words that imply more than "how adorable."

I have come to loathe the words "cute" and "adorable." I can think of only a few instances where they haven't made me feel like a child of five. You see, disability and infantilization are intrinsically linked. It is hard to separate the people who think it's "cute" that I can do things by myself from the people who use it to describe my looks.

And it's not just about my personal aesthetic; it's about how blind people are perceived, and thus how we see ourselves.

Toph, in *Avatar: The Last Airbender*, is a blind Earthbender. I love Toph. Toph has an adaptive aid for a magical power. Toph is snarky like me. But there is one moment that Toph really disappoints me, when she says about beauty: "One of the good things about being blind is that I don't have to waste my time worrying about appearances. I don't care what I look like. I'm not looking for anyone's approval. I know who I am."[7]

This is, honestly, such bullshit. I know some fully blind people who do not care about what they look like, but this is far from universal. Most of us take care and pride in our appearance. In fact, I know many blind people who worry about being the blind person who looks disheveled.

As with everything else in this book, blind people are caught up in a terrible trap: if we dress well, people assume we aren't really blind or that someone is helping us to keep up appearances.

---

7 *Avatar: The Last Airbender*, season 2, episode 15, "The Tales of Ba Sing Se," aired September 26, 2005, on Nickelodeon.

If we don't, we're dismissed, considered confirmation that blind people are useless and slovenly. There is no winning.

So I choose floral dresses and heels. If I'm going to lose, I might as well lose in petticoats. And I do lose, because by choosing the gender presentation that I am most comfortable in, I find myself in near-constant danger.

9.

The Call Is Coming
from Inside the House

Surviving Ableist Violence
Through the Lens of Horror

I don't know a single disabled woman or disabled nonbinary person who would not have to write the chapter that you are about to read. If I could, I wouldn't write it. I wouldn't write it because it hurts, but in memoir we have to tell the truth, and sometimes the truth is more difficult to share than you imagine.

In the United States, one in five women will be sexually assaulted in their lifetime.[1]

And while this statistic is itself terrible and unconscionable,

---

1 Statistics on nonbinary people are more difficult to come by because unfortunately queerness is often not thought of when we start to talk about assault and abuse. For more on *that* topic, read *In the Dream House* by Carmen Maria Machado.

we need to address the following: it's still an *if* for nondisabled women, especially nondisabled white women. For disabled women, especially for Deaf women, especially for disabled women of color, it is a *when*.[2]

Eighty-three percent of disabled women will be sexually assaulted in their lifetime, in some form.[3] And we are also more likely to experience intimate partner violence.[4]

---

2 Kathleen C. Basile, Matthew J. Breiding, and Sharon G. Smith, "Disability and Risk of Recent Sexual Violence in the United States," *American Journal of Public Health* 106, no. 5 (May 2016): 928–33, https://doi.org/10.2105/ajph.2015.303004. For women and men, having a disability was associated with an increased risk of sexual coercion and noncontact unwanted sexual experiences.

3 "Sexual Abuse," Disability Justice, January 27, 2018, https://disability justice.org/sexual-abuse/. When I say "in some form" I mean that there are many ways to be sexually assaulted.

4 Matthew J. Breiding and Brian S. Armour, "The Association Between Disability and Intimate Partner Violence in the United States," *Annals of Epidemiology* 25, no. 6 (June 2015): 455–57, https://doi.org/10.1016/j .annepidem.2015.03.017. Compared to women without a disability, women with a disability were significantly more likely to report experiencing each form of intimate partner violence (IPV) measured, which includes rape, sexual violence other than rape, physical violence, stalking, psychological aggression, and control of reproductive or sexual health. For men, significant associations were found with respect to stalking and psychological aggression by an intimate partner.

I am in the 83 percent. I am in the 50 percent of deaf girls who have been abused. I am numbered in the statistics that make my stomach churn and that make me want to scream. I want so desperately for this to be a series of shocking statistics that you need to walk away from it, just to process.

But of course, it's not. It is, instead, completely expected.

The experience of being victimized, the horrifying reality of knowing that what has happened to you once will almost assuredly happen again,[5] is what many disabled women live with daily. I know I do.

The horror genre uses that knowledge to victimize and revictimize us on-screen. Literature and film depict disabled women's bodies as vulnerable spaces to claim and destroy over and over again. It makes some movies nearly unwatchable for me, because even if there's no sexual violence between the villain and a disabled woman because she is deemed undesirable,[6] the camera is focused on the victimization of her disabled body.

The film *In Darkness* follows a woman pretending to be blind;[7] she's on a revenge quest, prepared to murder the man who raped and killed her mother. As it turns out, the villain has a penchant for raping and murdering not only women but also

---

5 Of that 83 percent, 40 percent will be victimized again. And again. And again.

6 In chapter 10, we'll talk about desirability politics, but they don't belong in the same chapter.

7 One of the few tropes I can't replicate on my own, covered in chapter 7.

blind women in particular. And that's not even what set off my trauma brain.

Forty minutes into the film, there is a sequence that made me want to crawl underneath a blanket and never come out again. Sofia is walking down a dark street somewhere in London.[8] She approaches a group of loud and drunk men on a dark street.

"Look where you're going, are you fucking blind or somethin'?" the first man shouts when she stumbles into them.[9] "Fuckin' hell, she *is* blind!"

This is when I tense up, when the hairs on the back of my neck stand on end. They corner her against a wall, they mock her when she asks to be left alone. And then they say the words that make me stop the film, so that I can breathe. "When was the last time you got fucked? Been a while, yeah?"[10]

She bats him away, the actress pretending she can't see where

---

8 As with other nondisabled and sighted actresses who play blind women, Natalie Dormer is no exception. She keeps her head straight, uses sharp head movements to indicate extreme listening, and her cane isn't nearly long enough to do its job properly.

9 When I hear a group of drunk men ahead of me I do not stumble into them. I navigate my way to another part of the street. This is the first instance of horror making disabled women have bad decision-making in order to victimize us.

10 The assumption that disabled people do not have sex is so pervasive that it is often used as a weapon. We'll enjoy being raped because we haven't had any in a while. We won't mind. We do, in fact, mind.

his hands are coming from. It is a classic trope, the blind woman incapable of defending herself, set upon by violent men, ready to violate her because they *can*. And they do. In shadow, we watch as they throw her to the ground; we hear a slap; there is a scream. "Are you on your knees already, love?" And as she cowers on the ground, someone else moves in and saves her.

The movie moves on, we do not see her react to the experience—and at the end of the film, when it turns out she was sighted all along, I have to admit, I am angry—because not only did the film perpetuate the victimhood of blind women but so did the main character.

I have been followed, I have been stalked, I have had men describe the things they wanted to do to me on a street corner.

And yes, more than that has happened, too.

In the television show *In the Dark* (which we discussed in chapter 6) the wildly unlikable and not very accurate main character Murphy is trauma bonded with her friend Tyson, who rescued her from a violent mugging. When he dies, it is the impetus for her to go and solve his killing. Because he rescued her.

In *Wait Until Dark*, a blind woman is the victim of a home invasion by thieves seeking a doll that has secretly been stuffed with drugs (or jewels, depending on the version). *Wait Until Dark* is a spiritual sequel to *Gaslight* in so many ways. Men need to remove a precious object from a woman's home, so they use whatever means necessary to render that woman unsafe. In the case of *Gaslight*, it is a husband terrorizing a wife into disbelieving her own senses, while in *Wait Until Dark*, it is the blindness of the victim that is used to create danger.

In *Hush*, a Deaf woman lives in the woods by herself and is the victim of a home invasion. I've never finished watching the film because of how carefully the filmmakers used the main character's Deafness to victimize her, how they weaponized her Deafness against the audience, too. Using it to strike chords of fear in our hearts.

Why are abled people so fascinated by the terror of disabled women? Why are there so many films that hinge upon watching a disabled woman fight for her life? Why is disability so rarely seen as a strength in horror and sci-fi?

Personally, I think the draw for abled people (conscious or otherwise) in making and watching this kind of entertainment is to reassure themselves that such horrible things will not happen to them. They would hear the killer on the roof. They would see the murderer coming around the corner. They could run away from the person trying to kill them.

The supremacy of ability is terrifying, because it presses forward the idea that a disabled person is an easy target, a good victim. Films like *Hush* and *Wait Until Dark* give the impression that even though a disabled person might have survived awhile, we're easily targeted.

It reinforces a stereotype that harms us in real time.

———

I never know where to start with my own victimization. Do I start with the molestation that was a steady experience throughout my childhood? Do I start with the incident that made me speak out to a therapist in high school, the one that leaves me with PTSD? Do I start with my own stranger-danger story? I never know, because I don't know what people will believe. Which part will cause them to stop listening and start getting up in their own feelings.

Most instances of disabled terror we see on the screen or read in a book occur at the hands of a stranger. A criminal spots a disabled person who can be taken advantage of. And technically, it's true that I am less safe on a city street than the average nondisabled person. But in reality, most disabled victims—just like abled ones—know their abusers.

The people who we are supposed to be able to trust—our caretakers, our partners, our lovers, our family members—those are the people who most often take advantage of our disabilities.

Horror is missing the fucking point.

Disabled children are murdered by their parents with staggering frequency.[11] Disabled people are assaulted by their partners and find themselves with nowhere to go, nowhere to hide. After

---

11 "Media Coverage of the Murder of People with Disabilities by Their Caregivers," Ruderman Family Foundation, September 25, 2017, https://rudermanfoundation.org/white_papers/media-coverage-of-the -murder-of-people-with-disabilities-by-their-caregivers/. Approximately once a week, a disabled person is murdered by their caregiver in the United States.

all, the people who know *exactly* how disabled we are are in the best position to exploit it.

And they do.[12]

The call is almost always coming from inside the house.

————

"Most forms of domestic abuse are completely legal."[13]

Gatsby never hit me. It's important for you to know that, because when most people hear *abusive marriage*, that's the first thing they think. In fact, he never raped me, either. He never hurt me in the ways that you are imagining. But he did hurt me. Deeply.

In the arbitration of a marriage there are only two memoirists, and in the aftermath of a divorce, you'll only ever hear the history of one side.[14]

My marriage had been slowly curdling, by degrees, over the last five years (out of eight). I'd thought maybe we could get

————

12 The Bureau of Justice Statistics did research between 2009 and 2015, indicating that "a higher percentage of violence against persons with disabilities (40%) was committed by persons the victims knew well or who were casual acquaintances than against persons without disabilities (32%)." But in terms of anecdotal evidence, this is only based on reported data, and community data is just as important.

13 Carmen Maria Machado, *In the Dream House: A Memoir* (Minneapolis: Graywolf Press, 2020).

14 Unless you know both parties and hear both perspectives . . . but even then . . .

through it, but it became progressively clearer that we weren't just on different pages of a book, we were in different genres. I was somewhere in the pages of a Virginia Woolf or Jessica Mitford novel and he was in a David Foster Wallace doorstopper.

I can chart our marriage through literature, describing it for the outsider in the books that we loved, my favorites and his.

The beginning of our relationship was like a spiky Evelyn Waugh novel: the delightfully quirky Deafblind historian who studied sex workers' legal rights marrying the misfit lawyer with a sarcastic sense of humor. We drank the right cocktails; I wore the right clothes. Toward the end, we had shifted. He was now afraid of Virginia Woolf, afraid of the things we couldn't speak about. The underlying discord that could never be voiced, except in explosive fights that would go unresolved for years. We were an Edward Albee play written years too late.

Abuse comes in many forms. When one partner is disabled, it might look like a house bought far from the gates of community support, like refusing to give a ride when it was needed, like refusing to communicate honestly and with kindness. It is silence when there should be support, and rage directed at you when you never said a word.

There was never anything to report. Never anything to tell the police. Never anything that could have required a restraining order. Yet I'm afraid of him. I am afraid of the silence that was filled with his rage. Afraid of the feeling that I had lying next to him in the dark when he was angry with me. The cold silence that never manifested as anything more than dismissal.

I have had abusive partners who did all the things that we assume that an abusive partner does.

But it was the pernicious and systemic damage of my ten-year relationship with my husband that did the most harm. It made me small, and afraid. It made me question whether I could survive without him.

Turns out, I survive without him just fine.

Before there was Gatsby, though, there was Holden.

I met Holden in my freshman year of college. We didn't date until my senior year, when I was newly out of a long-term relationship, and lonely. He flirted, he texted, he made me feel wanted. He treated me with desire; he took care of me when my body was a disaster zone. Where some people see pictures of us and think how happy we looked together, I see the possessiveness and the anger that colored our relationship.

Holden used my PTSD, my blindness, and my hearing loss to consistently trap me. He would grab me from behind corners, he would tell me that no one would ever love me like he did. And he told me the lie that haunts me to this day: that no one would ever want me like he did. He reminded me that he loved me while also doing everything that he could to strip me bare, to leave me without a single shred of spine, to make sure that my ability to say no was so compromised that he could take advantage when he wanted. Even after we broke up, he talked me into having sex with him. Even after we broke up, he would send me filthy text messages, trying to convince me that we should still be together.

He used every possible advantage that he had against me, and

I knew down in the deepest parts of my soul that if I told anyone—that if I went to the police, if I made a fuss, if I did anything to save myself—I would be told that I was disabled and I was lucky that someone wanted me.

I'd been told for years that the bullies who made middle school a living hell just "liked" me. That it was a boy's way of showing affection. That I should be grateful.

That I should be glad someone wanted me. After all, boys don't make passes at girls who wear Coke-bottle glasses. Or hearing aids.

It is this lie that creates a trap. A trap that makes us stay, even in bad partnerships with dangerous people, because we're sure no one else will want our broken bodies.

The message of "be grateful" is what victimizes us most. Because it makes disabled people feel like the only love they will ever receive is the love that comes with the monsters that lurk under the bed.

However, there is another side to the horror disability trope. When we aren't the perfect targets, easy to pick off, we are the monsters that lurk in the dark.

In *Scream*, the 2015–2019 television series based loosely on the film series of the same name, the main villain is murdering people because he couldn't get a prom date. Because he is disabled. While I'll admit that it was hard for me to get a prom date, and my experience of school dances was chiefly standing alone and slightly miserable in a pretty dress, no part of me wanted to violently murder my classmates.

Disabled bodies are often used to code for evil. Little people are conspirators, blind women are seers, even blind weapon masters inspire a certain amount of fear alongside respect. Fear imbues the disabled body, both in terms of nondisabled people wanting to avoid ever being like us, but also because we've been coded as scary. In *Don't Breathe*, a blind man is the victim of a home invasion, but unlike *Hush*, the Big Bad is not the invaders. It's the blind man himself. He never even has a name, because he is an archetype of evil.

In another classic disability trope, his super hearing allows him to sneak up and kill people in his home—and when the home invaders discover that he is not only a super-hearing blind man but also a rapist, the depiction really goes sour.

The Blind Man doesn't even rape women himself. The Blind Man rapes women with a turkey baster full of his own semen. This really underscores the issues plaguing disabled people when it comes to sexuality. There is something about the idea that a blind rapist cannot actually use his own penis that speaks to the larger issues of representation.

Don't Breathe was breathtakingly harmful because it used all the tropes—literally all of them—about blind people and used them to terrorize the nondisabled.

And when we are afraid of something, we are less likely to feel empathy for it. This is how racism works, this is how anti-Semitism works, and yes, this is how ableism works.

Fear breeds hatred, or at best indifference.

How do we, actual blind people, live in the world safely when we are caught between being victims (who are actually sighted and just pretending) and blind men who will kill you quick as a snake?

No one listens to us. Because in addition to being disabled, to having targets on our backs since day one, we've also been handed the curse of skepticism. Remember, all these people playing blind people are actually sighted. Remember, too, that blindness is defined in stark contrast to sight, so the sighted are the ones arbitrating whether we can be trusted.

As a disabled woman, I am not to believed. I can't see well enough, so the police don't feel I am a reliable witness. Someone else (my assailant?) would be needed to prove what happened to me. I can't hear well enough, so perhaps, the convention coordinator suggests, I *didn't hear him properly*. There could be no other reason for a deaf woman making a sexual harassment complaint.

As both a child and an adult, I have experienced the deepset gaslighting of the nondisabled world. I have learned time and time again that no matter how obvious an incident is, no matter how terribly I have been treated, I will not be believed unless there is a nondisabled witness to my trauma.

We are silenced by the disbelief of the abled. Our voices go unheard, yet we're depicted as the victims of a world that wants to watch us suffer. We are shown as the victims of home invasions, of assaults, of stalking. These problems are real—but in my experience, it doesn't make the audience more empathetic to the actual disabled people who experience them. In fact, the most authentic moment of *In the Dark* is when the police don't trust Murphy.

But every now and then, even horror can pleasantly surprise.

In 2018, the film *A Quiet Place* blew all my expectations of disability and horror out of the water. In it, a family of hearing people with one Deaf child (played by a Deaf actress) survives an apocalypse—and the primary reason for their survival is that they know ASL.

The moral of that particular story is that oralism[15] kills. For the first time in my life, I watched a narrative where disability wasn't the thing that would kill. It wasn't the reason for someone's victimhood. While I sat in a movie theater full of hearing people, their nervous giggles echoing in the space, I found myself moved to tears.

It was horror that was meant for me.

It gave me hope.

It gave me hope that I would be believed.

———

There has been a lot of pain in this chapter. A lot of sorrow. The reality is that disabled women are not safe, that the horror genre does demonstrate some truth, even when I hate that truth with every fiber of my being. And while the next genre on the list doesn't

———

15 Oralism is the theory that oral speech is better than all other forms of communication and must be enforced at all costs to the Deaf individual.

do much better (romance would also very much like it if disabled people didn't experience joy or pleasure), I'm pleased to report that if horror sometimes gets it right, romance is dead wrong.

As someone with PTSD, I have had to have the Talk[16] with a number of people. Sometimes the Talk goes well. Sometimes it is a conversation, a vulnerability that opens up to something more interesting. Sometimes it results in never getting another phone call. The Talk is partially about speaking the truths that no one wants to hear—acknowledging the horrible reality that I have experienced violence and pain. It is also about making sure that my history does not get erased.

The Talk is always a risk. The Talk is also partially telling a potential partner what they're getting into—they are dating someone with a target on their back, they are dating someone who might eventually be victimized *again*.

Most people, when we have the Talk, react with sorrow. They react with concern. Some don't know what to say. Some tell me about their own trauma in response. Mostly, the Talk is awkward and hard to manage, and I never quite know what to do once it's been had.

When I first moved back to Seattle in 2020, I lived on a houseboat. It was the very last house on the dock, the front deck liter-

16 The unfortunate conversation with a new partner where I inevitably have to tell them 90-ish percent of the bad shit that has happened to me so that they have a sense of what I can and can't do, whether it be in bed or otherwise.

ally hanging out onto Lake Union. The sunsets were spectacular; it was quiet and perfect. Just the right place to recover from a divorce.

In December 2019, I had gone on a first date. He was tall; he wore a lot of tweed. He was the kind of man who I looked at and thought, *Oh no, you're smart.* I knew he was trouble. Good trouble. But trouble nonetheless.

For three hours we sat on a couch in a Scotch bar, drank drams, held hands, and kissed. I mentioned that I had PTSD and said we would talk. He had it, too. He understood.

The Talk came in February, in the living room of that houseboat. He never said he was sorry, he never pitied me or behaved as though what had happened to me was either uncommon or too terrible to fathom. He didn't reach over to hold me.

He didn't expect me to make him feel better about the trauma. All he did was make sure I knew he believed me.

Reader, I'm still dating him. Remember Arthur from chapter 7?

10.

Cripping My Dance Card

Required Reading
for People Who Want to Date Me
(But My Relatives Should Skip to Chapter 11)

"I hope you don't mind me asking, but how much can you see and hear?"

The message sat in my OkCupid in-box, staring at me. She was the first person I'd matched with in a while. I'd been on a couple dates, had a few flirtations fizzle out. Pandemic Dating™ is hard and I didn't have a whole lot of hope. An hour after I saw the initial message, another popped up.

"I don't mean to be rude, but I'm being serious."

Serious about what? Certainly not about me. There was no indication that she thought I was cute, or that perhaps she'd want to go on a date with me. Just a question of whether I could see or hear enough for her liking.

I wondered, was this a factor of the pandemic, or was she simply yet another in a long string of people who were only willing to date me if I fit the criteria of able-bodied "enough" for government work?

It took me a really long time to figure out what this chapter needed to be about. I couldn't decide if it was about sex, or if it was about love, or if it was about the romance genre, or if it was about how lonely being disabled is, or if it was about beauty standards. I couldn't decide if it was about how the media both denies disabled women the ability to be seen as sexual beings, wanting us to stay virginal and childlike, and also paints us as sluts. Isn't the irony fun?

Honestly, I could write a whole book about the politics of desire and disability.[1] At the center of everything, the way that society treats disabled women is different from the way it treats disabled men and from the way it treats nondisabled women.[2]

Remember, society has already decided that we're victims. Despite saying that disabled women are not attractive, that we should not bear children, we are also victims of sexual abuse— there is still something worth taking from us.

The relationship that I have to my body has been shaped by nondisabled opinion across the board, and it is no more evident than when I think about sexuality and sex, romance, and dating.

Every time that I was told I was lucky that someone made a

---

1 Someday I will.

2 Yes, this chapter is treating things from a binary gender lens. Trans and nonbinary experiences of disability are outside of my lane, which we talked about in chapter 8.

pass at me, every time I was informed that it was rare that someone would see past my disabilities in order to take an interest,
made it just a little bit harder to trust that someday, I would be
loved for who I am and for the body that I live in.

In August 2019 I found myself on Arthur's Seat, in the middle
of Edinburgh. Astra led me all the way up the beautiful craggy
landscape, almost to the top. We stopped when it became a rock
scramble instead of a steep climb, working in tandem to reach
what I hadn't been able to seven years before, on my honeymoon.

Gatsby had been impatient the whole way. In fact, his frus-
trated energy had been present the entire time we were in Europe.
I could feel it in the way he walked ahead of us throughout Scot-
land, in the way he didn't really want to stand and chat with my
friends the day after I won a Hugo Award.[3]

It was at the top of Arthur's Seat, looking out over the city
of Edinburgh, that I promised myself I wouldn't be married in a
year. I didn't know if I would have to leave, or if we could come to
a mutual understanding, or what. But something would have to
change.

My disability had become a burden very clearly.

On the way down, I knew I had to commit this moment to

---

3 The Hugo Awards are given to science fiction writers for a variety of
achievements. I was the first blind woman to win one, and most certainly the first Deafblind person ever to win one.

memory as a part of my promise: the insistent pull of a Labrador nearly yanking me to the ground, and a husband already so far down the trail that I lost him in the sea of green grass and heather below.

His impatience, his lack of care . . . it was all I had believed I deserved, as a disabled woman. To be merely tolerated. And I'd had enough.

Five months later, I was single.

I found myself constructing a dating profile in December 2019 on OkCupid and contemplating for the first time in a decade how I wanted to manage the complexities of dating while disabled. I had made mistakes the last time. I'd been coy about disabilities when I shouldn't have been; I hadn't known all the right adaptive tools; I hadn't wanted to insist on partners learning some sign language when they should have. This time would be different.

The resulting profile was coy about some things (I was getting divorced) but straightforward about others (I had a guide dog and wear hearing aids).

So, I installed OkCupid on my phone and started swiping. My stated intention was to go on some meaningless dates (my words). I matched with a few people, set up a couple of dates, went on a few more.[4]

---

4 The first was with a woman who was more interested in learning about my guide dog than about me, the second was with Arthur and I missed three phone calls making sure I wasn't dead because he was charming.

I find myself anxious before first dates. Will I be able to hear them? Will they recognize me so I don't have to awkwardly ask if I'm meeting them? Will they be surprised or, possibly worse, fetishy about my disabilities? Horror and romance are, at least for disabled women, not entirely dissimilar.

The possibility of violence is part of the danger in a first date. It takes time to trust that the people we want to see will be kind. But there's another type of horror: the horror of indifference. The realization that they don't think they can handle the hearing aids or the adaptive aids.

But let's go back to that other view for a second, not the one that results in people deciding you're not worth their time but the one where you are being sought out for your disabled body specifically.

Devotees are a subsection of the kink community who seek out disabled people as objects of sexual desire. Sure, they want the disabled body. Sure. They're open to and in fact *excited about* sex with a disabled body.

But this view, to me, suggests that the disability is more important than the person. That the idea of sex with a blind woman, or a wheelchair user, is the sexy part, and the person who lives in the disabled body is not. I have nothing against kink. What I have an issue with is kinks and fetishes that rely upon my disabled body being an object. It also results in nondisabled people assuming that having sex with a disabled person *is itself* a kink, rather than looking at sex with disabled people as sex with another person.

I have often heard from people who are *not* devos that I should go find someone who is "into that sort of thing."

It sequesters disabled sex within a fetish, rather than opening the door to disabled sex as mainstream.

I can't help thinking there's a part of sideshow history here, a bit of the underground, the hush-hush idea that a disabled person having sex isn't right or proper.

In a world where ableism is a radioactive force, finding love (or just sexual pleasure[5]) is damn near impossible without a lot of hard work. Both for you and with the people who care about you.

At times in my life I have been impossibly lonely. To some, that will come as a surprise. To the outside observer I probably appear relatively confident, aware of what I bring to the table as a partner. That has not always been the case. Whenever I thought about marriage, or even long-term partnerships, the specter of my grandparents' whispers about my aunt Mary would rush back, singing the chorus of "not good enough, not pretty enough, not

---

5 Casual sexual encounters seem so easy to me for able-bodied people. As though you can just make eye contact, read some body language, meet someone on Tinder or Grindr. The barrier to entry for casual sex for most disabled people is nil. I've literally never had someone say, "Want to come up to my room?" Every encounter is planned. Every partner is vetted. Every person I have ever had sex with has been known to me. Perhaps casual sex isn't a requirement, but it's something that disabled people are often unable to access because of ableism.

capable enough." Lies that had become truths through sheer repetition. Beliefs I would have to undo over decades.

What were the lies? Let's be direct.

I was too difficult to love.

I did not deserve sexual pleasure because of my disabled body.

My disabilities made me a burden unequal to nondisabled partners.

In order to find partners I would need to make myself small and accessible. Manage myself, never ask for help, never be a bother.

None of those things are true. Not for me. Not for any disabled person. What these lies do is cut disabled people off from affection, from physical pleasure, from social constructs that build community.

But these lies are reinforced not just by society, or our media, but by our educational systems, which teach sex ed to nondisabled kids badly but teach it to disabled kids not at all. There's nothing in sex ed about hearing aids in bed, or wheelchair sex, or safe sex for intellectually disabled or developmentally disabled people.

Nothing.

So even if we are having sex (and we are) we're certainly not having it safely.

That doesn't even get at how disabled bodies are viewed, however. In chapter 4, I took you through all the ways in which my body has been placed on display, whether it is viewed through a medical lens as an oddity, riddled with the effects of congenital rubella, or if it is viewed as an object of pity or revulsion on the street. Whether my body falls into those contexts, whether I am an object of overcoming or of sadness, the views allowed of my body do not remotely come within the lens of desire.

We so often view women's bodies as objects of desire; Laura Mulvey's theory of the male gaze even posits that it's nearly impossible for straight cis white men to do anything else.

But if a disabled body is consistently placed in a form of brokenness, of pity, removing any possibility for desire—what then happens to the disabled woman who seeks desire?

As a former burlesque dancer, I know that it takes work to capture the imagination of a whole room, to make them look at you, to truly look at you as more than just an act.

But when it comes to sexual partners, the work isn't mine to do. My partners have to learn to see me with a different lens. To view me not as breakable, or as pitiable, but as desirable. And that takes time.

I didn't want to do my whole dating history in this chapter, and I still don't. But I want to give you some snapshots to understand what this damage looks like on the personal level as well as in our made-up worlds. So let's start here: I started to date in high school. In most of the romance movies, books, and others, the disabled characters have acquired disabilities and remember dating pre-disability. I never had that experience.

I had spent so much time in the Victorian novels of Arthur Conan Doyle and the fantasies of Tamora Pierce and Diana Wynne Jones that I had not paid much attention to the dating rituals of the midnineties. Of course, it wouldn't have mattered. For non-disabled teens there is a plethora of media representation;[6] you sort of have a sense of what social conventions are, how you are expected to navigate the dating world. We learn social norms from what's in front of us, whether it's television or real, live people.

But there were no blind or Deaf kids dating ahead of me in school, and with the exception of Heather in *7th Heaven*, there were no Deaf girls being asked out on dates on TV, either.

She is spotted by Matt, the eldest son on *7th Heaven*, and he must ask her out on a date. He's so enamored with her attractiveness that he follows her home because he doesn't have her phone number. This is creepy, but welcome to the nineties, I guess? He doesn't know she's Deaf until he shows up on her doorstep[7] and her mother has to act as an interpreter. It is surprising to me that a television show from the mid- to late nineties actually shows a Deaf woman being flirted with by a hearing man.[8] I know this was probably my first introduction to a Deaf woman in media, yet I didn't remember her. Eventually, Heather and Matt break up, in part because she can't imagine marrying a hearing man, but their flirtation lasts for most of the series as a will-they-or-won't-they tease.

---

6 To a certain extent, chronically ill teens have it now with *The Fault in Our Stars*. But it is wildly flawed and difficult, so I don't think of it as good representation.

7 Sidenote: creepy. Don't do this.

8 It also happens in *The West Wing*, when Josh Lyman has a crush on Joey Lucas, the Deaf pollster played by Marlee Matlin.

Before *7th Heaven*, there was *Children of a Lesser God*. It's a film based on a play[9] that tells the story of a Deaf woman and a hearing man who fall in love. To make the politics a little more blunt: it is about a Deaf woman who is a janitor at a school for the Deaf, who falls in love with a speech pathology teacher who wants her to learn how to speak—because she's smart.[10] Audism is a hell of a drug.

Children of a Lesser God and 2017's *The Shape of Water* are spiritual cousins, much like *Gaslight* and *Wait Until Dark*. They use similar visual motifs—even down to the main characters having sex underwater. The difference is that James in *Children of a Lesser God* is a human monster—and an abusive one—where the fish god in the other is . . . a literal monster. There's always been something deeply unsettling to me about how disabled women must settle for monstrosity in their partnerships.

For a long time, I settled. I accepted whomever decided I was worth spending time with, rather than being selective. I thought that I wouldn't have choices.

For most of my adult life, I've been pressured to pretend that I am not as disabled as I am, to inform partners of as little as possible, until they are able to see that I'm not *that* disabled, that it won't take them work to be with me. That's why I tried to downplay my disabilities on my OkCupid profiles for so long.

---

9 Yep, *The Miracle Worker* and *Children of a Lesser God* are both film adaptations.

10 Oralism kills. Just not in the same way as in *A Quiet Place*. In this case, it's more of a slow death of the soul.

One man, after asking what kind of ambience I liked, unmatched with me when I answered honestly that with bilateral hearing aids I liked quieter environments. It's not just that I'm afraid that people will be shitheads, it's that I've already experienced it, and these are *minor* examples.

In many ways, online dating gives me a bit of an edge. I can weed out the ableist and overtly problematic before I bother with meeting people in person. I'm a Deafblind woman; even before I had the dog, there was a certain amount of "opt in" required. An ex of mine once called me a Prestige Class[11] girlfriend. At first I thought it was funny; after all, everyone acts like it's so much harder to date me than it is to date a nondisabled woman. But after a while, it started to wear on my heart. It shouldn't be perceived as so difficult. I shouldn't have to reassure people so much that I am not a burden.

Disabled people are constantly told that they are burdens, told that their existence in society alone is too much for everyone to bear. In *The Theory of Everything*, Stephen Hawking's wife, Jane Wilde, is heaped with praise and called a saint for marrying Stephen. The implication is that because she stands by the man she loves while his disease progresses, because she bears his children and cares for them, she must be incredibly brave, her life incredibly difficult. While certainly ALS is a disease that takes much from

---

11 In Dungeons and Dragons these are characters who require a certain number of levels to play.

people who have been nondisabled their whole lives, when these are the only love stories about disability that we are shown, how is anyone to know differently?

The perception is that being committed to and loving disabled people is harder than committing to nondisabled people. That no one would choose it unless they were overwhelmingly compelled.

Honestly, people also assume that nondisabled people don't date disabled people.

In 2010, when I first started dating Gatsby, I went to meet him after work. The next day, one of his coworkers told him he thought it was great that he was volunteering with the blind. Gatsby was amused, a little baffled. I was furious.

We'd been making out in the hallway not thirty seconds before the coworker walked past us. Volunteering? Is it really that rare to see a couple where one person is disabled and the other is not? I suppose it is. On Netflix's *Love on the Spectrum*, the couples shown are all autistic people dating each other; there is no inter-abled[12] relationship representation, despite it being perfectly common in the real world.

My nondisabled partners have lacked fluencies in experience that nondisabled people will never have. They will likely never

---

12 Many people find the term "inter-abled" problematic, and that's fair. But we don't have a lot of terms for nondisabled/disabled relationships, and there is an experiential divide that I think must be acknowledged.

quite understand the pain of being called disfigured on a three-hundred-person Zoom call.[13] Honestly, that's okay, they don't have to. They can learn about ableism in other ways. Eventually, they all do.

Two of my partners have dated disabled people before. I dated both of those people in 2020, when I started to really focus on what I needed out of relationships and not what I assumed I could get. I remember remarking to Arthur that I was unlucky, and he replied rather astutely that actually, it had to do with society.

He was right.

I have had to become comfortable with the fact that there will be people who don't want to date me because of my disabilities. It feels wrong, but ultimately the only goal is to be with people who see me for who I am. Allowing people to not be interested, instead of clinging to the possibility until someone gives in. It's true that society has made it more difficult for me to find love, to find partners, to find intimacy.

The responsibility for fixing that isn't on me. It's not on me to be less disabled or to only date other disabled people. No, it's the responsibility of everyone else on the app to choose to undo their own ableism.

The only promise I can make to myself is that I will never again try to argue someone into dating me, I will never be the sort of person who makes a convincing argument for dismantling ableism.

Do it on your own time.

---

13 No, really. That fucking happened.

In one particularly striking moment in *Children of a Lesser God*, Sarah—Marlee Matlin's character—says, "Sex was something I could do as well as hearing girls—better."[14]

It's so weird to me to see a Deaf character talk about sex so frankly, given that we rarely see disabled people have sex in most of our media. The handful of examples range from deeply offensive to abusive to raunchy—but there's little that actually models *how* to have sex with a disabled person. Let alone date them.

In *Switched at Birth*, Deaf teen characters make out and talk about having sex. They are not depicted as virginal or childlike. But there's none of the experiences that I have had baked in to make it feel authentic. And that's with Deaf actors there to check the hearing writers.

But of course, the reality is so much more complicated.

First, all these examples are of Deaf women. Deafness seems to occupy a sensual space when applied to femininity that blindness does not. Blindness is so often either clumsy or hyper-precise, but there's never a space for softness or sensuality. The few blind women in film and television who do have sex seem to have it in

---

14 Actually, James vocalizes this, while Sarah signs it. James speaks all of Sarah's lines as an interpreter for the audience, instead of the use of captions being provided. At first I thought that perhaps it was neat to have the ASL remain untranslated for the abled viewer—until it turned out the translation was there, just not as Sarah.

wild and imprecise ways, casually and with abandon. It's not that the sex they're having is bad, per se, it looks like fun. But it's also, again . . . not that realistic.

We see less blindness in sexuality representation because sighted people rely so much on their sight for sexual interaction. Deafness is easier to represent in the bedroom for hearing people, because they just think of it as quiet. But take away the visual, and they're lost.

Naturally, there are subtle differences in how we engage with and participate in sexuality, but there are also . . . less subtle ones. None of which ever makes it to the screen, stage, or page. Let me explain:

I'm wearing a black floral dress. It nips in at my waist, and the neckline dips down to show off my cleavage. The skirt is long enough that I can bend over, and the fabric is soft to the touch and inviting. It even has pockets. It's the perfect dress. The pink flowers mixed in with blue and white even match my hearing aids.

Arthur and I had been flirtatiously texting for a week. I had been thinking about the way his hand felt on my arm, about the implication that I shouldn't wear a cardigan . . . About that kiss at the end of our first date.

The dress was a deliberate choice. Of course I wore that dress. What else was I going to wear?[15]

---

15 At the time, I was living out of a suitcase, so, actually, it may have been my only option.

The minute our shoes were off, our coats were hung up, our bags were set down . . . the damn second the dog was off leash, we were like polarized magnets.

You couldn't have stopped us from kissing if you'd tried. First his hands went to my waist, then my neck . . . and then up to my face.

And my hearing aids squealed.[16]

Oh, you thought this was going to be hot crip sex? Sorry, I do nothing in this book without critical analysis.

When I go to bed with someone, there are factors that they may never have thought of before. The first is the obviously squealing hearing aids—they make themselves known. When they do, I have to ask if it's all right for me to take them out. Some people are uncomfortable with this—and honestly, they should be. I'm taking out a body part. I'm deadening one of my senses to go to bed with them. It takes more trust than most realize, and it is why I am picky about my partners. I have been led astray too many times by people who cannot be trusted. But we never see the conversation about whether the hearing aids should stay in—and it depends entirely on the type of hearing aid, anyway. (It's easier to have sex with in-the-ear hearing aids than behind-the-ears. Ask me how I know.)

After a while with a partner, I can understand them better

---

16 I've become adept at ignoring the aids in favor of staying in the moment.

without the aids in. It's about familiarity, a deepening of the relationship that takes time.[17]

The hearing aids are only the first step. The second step is my glasses. They're expensive, and I need them. I take those off, too. Not that sex has to be spectacularly athletic, but they get in the way.

So that's two senses down. At which point I'm in bed, not wearing clothes, with another person.

No hearing aids, no glasses. Just me. For some people, that's probably terrifying. There's some serious intimacy in being in what I sometimes think of as my natural state. The hearing aids, the glasses, it's all artificial. It's a way to get me on the same playing level as everyone else.

But the best part of connecting with a partner is the moment when I don't need to wear them anymore.

It's twofold. Firstly, that I have become accustomed to their voice, to their body, and to their presence enough that I don't feel the need to be hypervigilant. Secondly, they are comfortable enough with my disabled body that we no longer need that compensation. Learning how to exist alongside a disabled body is a process, too.

Romantic relationships with me are crash courses in critical disability theory. We have to break down ableist beauty standards, and explore complicated feelings about hearing aids and adaptive aids in the bedroom. I find myself explaining how to select a res-

---

17 This happens with distance vision, too. After a time, I start learning how to recognize people at a distance based on their gait, the colors they wear, the way that they approach me.

taurant for a Deafblind woman, what kinds of seating are better or worse for someone with a guide dog. I teach critical disability theory in my underwear, while holding hands, in OKCupid message threads, and through flirtation.

For a long time I didn't express what I needed in the bedroom because I was afraid of what my partners would think or feel.[18] I had a lot of sex that wasn't actually comfortable for me, I had a lot of make-outs where I didn't take out my hearing aids—or where I wasn't wearing them at all and didn't communicate what that meant I needed.

Consent gets fuzzy when you're driving in the Deaf lane. Most people don't really know what communication should look like with a disabled partner—or even what questions to ask.

That lack of awareness imbues our media. Yes, there are disabled characters having sex, but we never show the technical aspects. We don't get those conversations, I think, for two reasons: one, is that there are precious few disabled people writing about sex in our media, and the other is that nondisabled people are really uncomfortable with disabled people having sex. It comes back to that infantilization issue.

In 2020's *Come As You Are*, three disabled men go on a road trip to lose their virginities at a brothel in Montreal. For the record, these characters are all past the age of twenty-one, with the oldest character—a blind man—being thirty-five. Now, this is somewhat

---

18 I'm still working on this, still fighting past some of the stigma that haunts me.

believable in that much of the disabled community does have trouble accessing sexual experiences—especially in high school when emphasis on traditional beauty standards is part of the game played to lose ones virginity.

I recognize that there are many disabled people who both work as sex workers and who have visited sex workers, and that's not what I have an issue with. The problem is that the *primary* image of disabled people—specifically, disabled men—having sex is with sex workers.[19] It is more comfortable to associate disabled sex with an economic interaction than it is for nondisabled people to associate disabled sex with intimacy and love and desire. Most nondisabled people will laugh or say they would never, because they have fallen for all the traps that society has laid for them in viewing a disabled body as more than just a prop for various moral mental exercises.

The most disappointing part of *Come As You Are* is its ending. Not only do the disabled men have sex (in a fade-to-black moment where we get no visual of what they get up to—leaving abled audiences unclear, yet again, with how wheelchair users participate), but one of the three men dies the night after he loses his virginity.

While the blind character ultimately ends up with a girlfriend (deeming him at least somewhat deserving of romantic affection), I still find myself left cold by these depictions.

Of all the examples of the romance genre colliding with disabled peoples realities, *Me Before You* is the most nightmarish.

---

19 Another example is Netflix's *Special*.

Because at its core, the point of this movie is that the only good disabled partner is a dead one.

Louisa is an inexperienced caretaker[20] in desperate need of a job. Will is a quadriplegic billionaire with more money than God, a handsome face, and a fully accessible carriage house attached to his family's castle. Will has everything.

They begin to fall in love. She wears pretty dresses and sits on his lap in his wheelchair, and for a few moments, the disabled audience wonders if this will be the time we get to see a disabled man have sex on-screen.

It is not.

Instead of navigating the realities, their love story becomes a tragic one, ultimately ending with Louisa holding Will's hand in an expensive cottage in Switzerland where he can legally end his life.

They never have sex.

A few weeks later, she receives all the money that he had, a way to start a new life in which he will not burden her with his existence.

So in most romance movies and books, the main characters, you know, get it on. Fall in love. They marry. The point of these romance novels is to picture a fantasy in which the romance happens to you.

---

20 There is a whole genre of movies about inexperienced caretakers rolling in to save the day. Louisa has no experience, but because she's cute, she gets to take on the job anyway—because, as his parents say, maybe it will convince him to live.

So my question. My actual question is not *Why the fuck did this get published?* My question, dear reader, is: *Why the fuck is this categorized as romance?*

No, sex is not the point of a romance novel, though it certainly does play a central role in many of them. Typically, marriage is the central goal of the protagonist.[21] However, the idea that a romance novel is about a person dying and leaving someone money . . . that they've never even slept with . . . that tells me a lot about what we think of disabled people.

These days, most marginalized communities have at least some movies where they're depicted falling in love, and yet here, in the disability community, we have nothing. We have stories of dying and leaving the women we could have loved all our cash; we have stories where we fell in love with a monster because the world couldn't see us as human; we have movies where the only person we can love is hearing and abuses us for not using oral speech.

We get distinctly second-class love stories. Disabled people are told through fiction that if we are loved—and that's a big *if*—it

---

21   In the United States, disabled people are nearly entirely cut out of the social fabric of marriage because the financial supports afforded to disabled Americans are also tied to specific numbers. A disabled person cannot marry someone who will cut them off from their benefits in many circumstances. Imagine the romance novel: I can't marry you because I'll lose my Social Security Disability Insurance and my state-provided assistance!

will be despite our disabilities. We are told that love will probably not come for us, at least not romantic, will-you-share-your-life-with-me kind of love, no. Love will only come with obligation, with sacrifice, by playing down our disabilities. The media tells us that we are burdens, best left in a grave. That we are not loved.

But we *are* loved.

I have been loved for exactly who I am. Scars and blindness and Deafness and all. I have been desired with that body. I have been wanted and needed for it. But not just the physical aspects, though they are part and parcel of loving me. I have been loved for my mind. I have been loved for the person that I am. The disabled person that I am.

That's what all these movies, and books, and television shows get so exasperatingly wrong. They assume that for a disabled person to be loved they must supersede their body, that they must be more remarkable than their physical reality. That something else about them, preferably something extraordinary, must make the disabilities worth tolerating.

But no. I have been loved for precisely the person that I am. I'm not "too pretty" to be disabled, nor am I "too smart" or "too young." I'm who I am, and that's why the people who love me do. Not despite the body that I live in.

Perhaps that's the most radical act of them all. To love a disabled person, and for them to love you back, without ever asking them to change or to adapt better, just for you.

———————

Another date night, summer of 2020. Arthur and I are on my terrible beige couch. I'm somewhere in his lap, our feet are on the floor, practically sprawled onto each other because yes, it's a bad couch. Especially for this. I slide into his lap, leaning over to kiss him fully on the lips. His hands come up to my neck, and yes, my hearing aids shriek like a banshee.

I pull back, smirk, and pull out the aids. "Bedroom?"

He nods.

These are moments we don't see in media, or really, anywhere.

We don't hear those squealing hearing aids. Yet I experience them every time I move toward intimacy with someone.

We don't hear the chirp of a microphone when the heroine puts her head on her lover's shoulder, either. Yet they're always there when I snuggle.

We don't see a woman put her guide dog into a down-stay before she cups another woman's face in her hands and kisses her at the end of her going-away party. But I did that.

We don't see guide dogs on first dates, or white canes being swapped to off hands so that the lovers can hold hands while they walk together. But that's what happens every time Arthur and I go for a walk.

We don't hear husbands or partners gently say, "Watch out for that step,"[22] without fear of the blind woman tripping. But every partner I've ever been with has had to carefully stop me from falling on my face at least once. There is no road map for learning

---

22 Actually, Arthur says, "Could you not fall?" He wanted me to tell you that.

how to adapt to a disabled partner, because the dance hasn't been choreographed for you. Every couple will eventually chart their own.

We don't see blind women or wheelchair users performing burlesque. And yet, you can, if you look for it.

We don't see it because these visions of intimacy or desire are outside the realm of the nondisabled imagination.

Yet everything I've described has happened to me. They are all real, intimate moments. Reality is so much better than what media has gifted us.

There is love, and hope. There is desire. There is intimacy, emotional and physical. There is so much more than pity and despair.

So often we see disabled people on the outside of romance, looking wistfully for someone to love them for exactly who they are. But I won't be kept at arm's reach from the pleasure and intimacy that I desire and crave. I won't be stopped from dating the people I want to and from seeking out relationships that have meaning and depth.

Because I—and all disabled people—deserve it.

11.

Coming Out of the Closet

But Only If It's ADA Compliant

S o, as you may or may not have figured out, I'm bisexual.[1]
But in media,[2] there are no queer disabled women.[3]
What else is there to say?[4]

---

1 *Bisexuality* is the word that I use for myself. I do not define gender as two genders, because that's binarist, and as you may or may not have figured out by now, I hate binaries.

2 There is one gay disabled man in Netflix's *Special*, and there is a lesbian couple on *Switched at Birth*. It's not enough.

3 There are now. Marieke Nijkamp, Corinne Duyvis and many other YA authors in the disability space are creating them day after day after day. But those characters are sadly not in our mainstream media yet. They are still in niche spaces, and we need them out of the closet.

4 *So* much. But there is a whole book there. There is a whole series of books on the erasure of queer disabled identity. Because the queer

12.

There Are No Blind Moms on TV

Disability and Parenthood Stigma

"**L**ots of blind women have babies," says the blind mom on *Call the Midwife* (who is played by blind actress Ellie Wallwork). Yet the character's sister speaks all the horrible things that abled society likes to tell us: your baby isn't safe with you, you aren't capable of raising a child, what if the child is blind like you are? She turns her own sister in to social services because she believes being a blind mother is a cruelty to the child. *Call the Midwife* does what few television shows have done in the last thirty years: show a blind woman working toward parenthood with support and grace, fighting the ableism that surrounds her.

---

community was so traumatized by the AIDS pandemic, I think that is part of why the queer community has trouble creating space for disabled bodies. Sickness and disabled bodies remind the community too much of the pain of the 1980s.

I have wanted to be a mom for most of my life. I've cuddled my friends' children, told stories at bedtime, been terrified that my niece and nephew wouldn't like me. Until my aunt Mary got pregnant, I had never thought that my disabilities would prevent me from being a parent, but I quickly gleaned from my grandparents' furtive whispers that blind parents were viewed as irresponsible.

My grandparents had all these assumptions about how my aunt would parent, how she would even be capable of parenting. They talked about their worry as though praying; it almost felt like they wanted something terrible to happen so they would be right. I heard every word, and I internalized it. Judging her, before I realized that by doing so I was also judging myself.

As an adult, I would work at a preschool and nursery, carefully tending to infants and toddlers with the greatest of ease. Yes, babies and children are a challenge with blindness and deafness,[1] but unlike adults, children adapt. They learn. For the most part, they want to help.

In graduate school, my classmate Barbara—my first wheelchair-using classmate—wrote one of her papers on parenthood and disability. It was the first time in my life that someone I knew talked openly and honestly about how many barriers faced disabled women when it came to parenthood. She wrote of stories where children learned to crawl into their wheelchair-using parent's lap, of hearing children who signed with their Deaf parents.

---

1 Let's be honest with ourselves, they're difficult for nondisabled people, too.

It was the first time I thought it might be possible for me to parent. Before that, I'd more or less convinced myself that even though I was good with children, no one would want to coparent with me.

Now I had hope. Just a sliver. My internalized ableism told me that I wasn't *that* disabled, and that since it wasn't hereditary,[2] it didn't matter anyway.[3]

In 2015, I got pregnant. It wasn't planned. I'm still not entirely sure how it happened (but birth control is not 100 percent effective, kids).

I'd been very ill. We weren't entirely sure, but there was a possibility that I had MS. Something was wrong with my back. It turned out it was an effect from the way that my scar tissue pulls my body, but for a while there, we were scared.

In the hot summer of 2015, we went to Las Vegas. I'd gained some weight. I'd missed my period. One month. Then two. I called my doctor and asked about it, but they dismissed me, saying that with the pain I'd had it wasn't a surprise that my body was throwing punches.

The day I found out I was pregnant was the same day that I found out that I had lost my baby.

I *had* been pregnant. Past tense.

Even now, I remember that when I told Gatsby both that I *had* been pregnant, and that we weren't going to be parents, he

---

2 This, too, is internalized ableism by the way. The idea that disabled people shouldn't pass on their disabilities. But I had to learn.

3 Perceptions change. Now I think I'd make a kick-ass mom.

was so relieved about that latter that he couldn't engage with the part where it hurt me. Emotionally and physically, it hurt me very deeply. He was silent, awkward. Unable to talk to me about what had happened.

But while he wanted to hide it away, to forget that I had ever been, for a fragmentary moment, with child, there were realities my body and I had to face.

A miscarriage is not just a bad period. There are details to attend to.

So I went to the doctor. She did a scan, a small procedure. She told me I was going to be fine.

I was not fine.

Somehow in the back of my head I knew this was probably the only pregnancy I'd ever have—and I hadn't wanted it to end, even if I hadn't known it was there to begin with.

It was then, in the sterile room, wearing a paper gown, that the conversation turned to eugenics.

"It's normal for women like you to have a hard time conceiving." She said, patting my hand a little. "You know, it's probably just as well. I'm sure you want a healthy baby."

I was in a bit of a haze, but after a moment I realized what she was saying.

"Oh, no. That's not . . . ," I started to say, beginning to spin up the dialogue on how my disability wasn't *like that* before catching myself and refusing to throw my fellow disabled people under the bus. "It's not hereditary" is what I think I landed on.

She clearly didn't hear me. My voice was probably barely above a whisper anyway.

"I'm surprised you were able to get pregnant, given your conditions. With the difficulty you've had with your cycles, you know I'd be happy to offer you surgical options."

I remember my world went hot. She was offering to sterilize me, with a kindly smile on her face. She was offering to sterilize me, quite cheerfully, when I was clearly distraught at the idea that I had been pregnant and *had no fucking clue.* She was offering to sterilize me because in her mind, a disabled woman shouldn't have a baby.

I have friends who are child-free, friends who cannot stand the idea of being in the same room with an infant, or even a grown child. They shudder at the idea of children.

Do you know what no doctor will ever offer them? What no doctor in a thousand years will allow them?

A tubal ligation, an ablation, a hysterectomy. For them it is a long line of visits with psychiatrists, papers signed that say their husbands are all right with never having children. They hear a thousand "but what-ifs" and "but you might change your minds."

But me? Mere minutes after being told I'd lost a baby—one that I would have very much wanted—they were ready and willing to offer me surgical measures to make certain I'd never become a biological parent.

We all know what that means. No one wants more disabled babies.

———

I'm not going to be a bio mom at this point. I'm sure it could happen, but there are factors that make it more difficult. For one, I'm not signing up for single parenthood. I need a village, or at best a partner, willing to carry part of the load.

If I'd chosen to go that route I would likely not be approved for adoption because the system actively discourages disabled people from parenting. While it shouldn't be, often there is an unsaid requirement that you must be nondisabled in order to be considered.

As I've watched those doors and windows close, as I've recognized them for what they are, I have had to mourn.

That miscarriage was my only shot at parenting a child who looks like me from the very beginning of their life.

I've come to be fine with that.

I am an excellent aunt. My niece Jessica[4] fell asleep in my arms the first time I met her. She lets me hold her and doesn't reach for her parents. By the time I've published this book she'll be three and I won't have seen her for nearly two years because of the pandemic.

It aches. But even more painful is that, when I am with my niece in public, no one assumes that I am her mother. Generally, if a woman in my age bracket is holding a baby, she's told that the baby is adorable and congratulations.

That . . . does not happen to me.

———

4 Named for Jessica Mitford.

Society actively discourages blind women from being mothers. In media, we have few examples of disabled families, *especially* disabled mothers.

Switched at Birth provides us with Melody Bledsoe, tough Deaf mom, activist, and ex-wife. Melody is an interesting character because she is often the foil to the lead hearing character, Bay, girlfriend of Emmett.

Melody doesn't approve of Emmett being with a hearing girl; she strongly prefers that he date a Deaf girl. We see her parent teens with strength and compassion. But one of the challenging things about Melody is that while she is a Deaf mom, she has already raised a toddler, an infant. We don't see her momming in the way that many nondisabled moms are portrayed in media. We never, for example, see her hold a baby. In a romance plot with Gabe, the audiologist, he wants to adopt babies with Melody—but the birth parents ultimately don't agree. A lost opportunity, in my opinion, to see a disabled person become a mother.

The only other disabled mother I could find in television history is Mary Ingalls, in *Little House on the Prairie*. In real life, Mary did not have children. She lived with family, grateful for whatever care they gave her. But in the television show she *does* parent, including babies and small children.

I often wish that we had more representation like this— because the assumption that a blind woman won't have children, and the dialogue around Deafness and having children, is consistently focused on the concept of heritability.

And *that* is rooted in eugenics.

One of the first conversations that I had with my ex-mother-in-law was about whether or not her grandchildren (whom she expected me to bear for her) would be disabled like I was. I didn't ask if she would love them less if they were, but just the fact that we were discussing it made me feel very deeply that she would.

In that same graduate school class where Barbara and I talked about the societal expectations of disabled mothers, I also experienced the first public interrogation of my childbearing capability.

My class on the History of the Body was discussing how different marginalized bodies experienced different expectations. Somehow we'd come around to disabled bodies and disability, and one of my classmates said in front of everyone, "But you can't have kids, can you?"

It's a more common question than you might think. (Or maybe you've caught on, at this point in the book, that disabled bodies are public property.)

Alexander Graham Bell, inventor of the telephone, didn't want Deaf people to have children, because he believed that the creation of a Deaf race was a bad thing. He believed that society should eradicate Deafness as a human trait.

But why? Why is Deafness so awful?

When people ask if my children are going to be like me, they're asking with trepidation. They're not asking if my children will grow up to be writers or activists. They're not asking if they will have gray eyes or dark brown hair; they are asking if they will have cataracts and wear hearing aids. If they will suffer from chronic pain or post-traumatic stress disorder.

I almost wish the answer was yes.

But it's not. My children would never inherit my disabilities because my disabilities are a freak accident, a birth defect caused by external illness, not by a so-called flaw in my DNA.

Conversations about children are also where I often catch the subtle whiff of ableism, the fear of contagion. I've watched as people hand their babies over to small children, while subtly not choosing to let me hold their baby because they're afraid I'll drop them.

Disabled women are not expected to be mothers. Nor are we expected to get married.

The fundamentally restrictive heteronormative patterns of life aren't applied to disabled women. When Helen Keller wanted to marry her beau, her family—and Anne Sullivan—wouldn't let her. While Mary Ingalls may have married and had children in the television show, she was barred from it in real life.

In the United States in 1927, we had *Buck v. Bell*.[5]

Carrie Buck was an intellectually disabled[6] white woman who lived in an institution in Virginia. She was also the victim of government-sanctioned sterilization. Justice Oliver Wendell Holmes memorably defended the fact that she was sterilized by saying that "three generations of imbeciles is enough."

Ableism and eugenics are enshrined into our legal history. It

---

5 "*Buck v. Bell*," Oyez. Accessed March 1, 2021. https://www.oyez.org /cases/1900-1940/274us200.

6 The text of the case refers to her as "feeble-minded."

took the court two weeks to decide that a disabled woman being sterilized against her will was not a violation of her constitutional rights.

The truth is, the United States *is* a eugenicist country. Not only did this decision affect the agency of women all across the United States, it also traveled around the world. Nazi medical doctors used the case law of *Buck v. Bell* to defend themselves at the Nuremberg Trials.[7] Think about that for a second: actual Nazis used a Supreme Court case to say it was okay to kill and sterilize Jewish people and disabled people as part of the Holocaust.

The United States structurally supports sterilization of disabled women, Black women, and women of color, so of course our society doesn't think of disabled women as capable of having children.

And it's *still happening here.*

In September 2020, a nurse working for ICE blew the whistle on a doctor nicknamed "the Uterus Collector,"[8] who was sterilizing migrant women without their knowledge or consent. I watched

---

7 Harry Bruinius, *Better for All the World: The Secret History of Forced Sterilization and America's Quest for Racial Purity* (New York: Vintage Books, 2007).

8 Nick Miroff, "Hospital Where Activists Say ICE Detainees Were Subjected to Hysterectomies Says Just Two Were Performed There," *Washington Post*, September 22, 2020, https://www.washingtonpost.com /immigration/ice-detainee-hysterectomies-hospital/2020/09/22/aaf2 ca7e-fcfd-11ea-830c-a160b331ca62_story.html.

as nondisabled people yelled about how wrong it was, how un-American. I watched as people forgot that the United States is actually the originator of eugenics, and that if the doctor treating me after my miscarriage had wanted to, she could have decided that I *needed* to be sterilized and done so without my consent.

Because it is still legal to practice eugenics in the United States. There is limited legal recourse for disabled women or women of color to assert bodily autonomy.

Buck v. Bell is still on the books, and we have been begging to have it overturned for nearly a century.

I have heard other disabled women talk about how they have been offered hysterectomies, told by their doctors that they shouldn't have more children, had it implied that it would be better if they chose not to.

There is no support system for disabled women to make families.

It's not merely that disabled women don't have children; it's that we are assumed not to have *families*. So often, that we are only perceived as being "family" within the context of being cared for.

It's what made Heather's appearance in *7th Heaven* so very remarkable. A Deaf woman on television who appears in a wedding gown, who talks about having Deaf children, all of it within the context of a hyper-Christian liberal television show.

Being disabled and queer means that I've put great stock into the tradition of chosen family. For many people who are disabled, their blood families have failed them in one way or another. They have been told that their bodies make them useless, or that they are unworthy of family ties. They are treated as burdens. As a result, they need new systems for care.

As someone raised by the queer community of Seattle and Brooklyn, I have always known the value of chosen family. When I talk about my family it doesn't only include ties of blood or bonds of marriage.

Queer family is such an important component of disabled communities. We bury each other when there is no one left to mourn us, we throw birthday parties and send housewarming gifts, we host each other for holidays, and we open our doors when people have been rejected.

Disability is much the same. I think a lot about how the disabled community and the queer community have so much in common and yet don't always integrate well. At the end of the day, I think some of it is intergenerational trauma. The queer community has long excelled at caring for each other, especially during the AIDS crisis.

But the place where nontraditional family structures have benefitted me most have been as a disabled woman. My nuclear family is small, but my community, the people I consider family, is large. I have brothers and sisters, nieces and nephews, aunts and uncles. I have family that has been adopted through support structure and family that has been adopted through faith.

Now that COVID is here, I find we are all adapting to new ways of being family. Seders are conducted over Zoom (I went to four in 2020, a record for me). So are birthday parties and meeting the

parents. While the world feels in many ways more distant, the tradition of found family has become even more important.

So, no. I might not be a mom. I find that ache eases because
I am a part of a community that lets me have access to children,
access to family, access to a network that cares.

So often, the impulse to have children in a heteronormative,
nondisabled world is assumed to be so that there will be someone
to take care of you at the end of your life. I have never had to worry
about that. Someone will be there, waiting for me at the end of
my days. There will be people to say mourner's kaddish for me, to
wrap me in my tallit, and to put me in the dirt.

Breaking out of the heteronormative paradigm is a part of the
disabled experience.

Yet all the television shows, all the movies, all the books, insist that disabled people should be viewed in nondisabled, heteronormative family structures.

Except in horror, where things occasionally get interesting.
In both *Bird Box* and *A Quiet Place*, interdependence becomes a
value for survival. In *A Quiet Place*, the family has developed cop
ing mechanisms that actually rely on their Deaf daughter speaking
ASL. They have learned the values of silence and interdependence
before the film even starts, and it is those skills (creating sand
pathways, bright alarm lights, and more) that protect them.

In *Bird Box* we see it very briefly, but the end of the book and
the film both acknowledge that in an apocalypse where not being
able to see the monsters becomes an advantage, the blind community bands together and creates safety where there was none

before. It is possible to create community that is built on disability as a proper safety net.

Which is why disabled people can and should be parents. Being a parent is about creating safety, and safety is something that disabled people must create for themselves every day.

———

Back to that doctor's office in New Jersey, where I sat with a paper gown and an empty womb. The doctor bustled about the room, going over my charts, discussing my menstrual histories, the fact that I have migraines, and there was some concern over the type of birth control that I used. After she had offered to sterilize me I asked her why she was willing to give me such a procedure, when so many people I knew wanted it and didn't receive that care.

At first she didn't want to answer me.

At first she didn't want to reply, but I pressed until she quietly said that it was in light of my "conditions" that she thought perhaps I wouldn't want to pursue a pregnancy. That maybe I'd be "better off" adopting.

It is embedded in our society, the idea that disabled people do not want to carry a child to term, that our bodies will dispense more disabled bodies. That we should not perpetuate the evil stepmother's curses that have been laid upon us.

We are told by society not to desire motherhood. Because it's too dangerous, because we are not enough.

I never got a chance to find out what it would be like to be a Deafblind parent—I certainly don't know of any in fiction, or even in history. Helen Keller's own family didn't allow her to marry or have children, so why should my life be any different?

But that's the ableism talking.

The medical profession clearly enforces the standard that disabled bodies are not worth reproducing. We see this in developments of technologies like CRISPR[9] and in the choice to offer a healthy disabled woman sterilization.

Which is why we have to talk about the medical community and what they've done to disabled people onstage, on-screen, and in reality. It is doctors who made the decision to enact the horrors of eugenics; it is the doctors who make our bodies problems to solve; it is the medical-industrial complex that ultimately is to blame for so much of the antidisability rhetoric that we see in modern society.

---

9 CRISPR is a technology designed to allow doctors to edit the DNA of a fetus before they are born, in order to eradicate things like disease, Down syndrome, or the less malignant brown eye.

13.

I Am Not a Teaching Tool

Medicalizing the Disabled Body

When I was born, my parents were thrown, unprepared, into a high-stakes medical drama. My ophthalmologist wanted to perform surgery after surgery, acting as though he needed to "win" by making me sighted. My infant pediatrician told my parents to put me in an institution, give me up, and have another one.

· I was the star of a *Grey's Anatomy* episode, shrouded in tents and plexiglass cases, fighting to survive.

The medical profession looks at my body as a problem to be solved, rather than a patient to be treated, and I have felt that through my entire life. Every new doctor appointment is an exercise in concern. I arrive with sheafs of paperwork, armed with a pen and my medical history, ready to argue every point and fight for every ounce of care that I need.

I come with a medical history that starts before I was even out of the womb.

For five years, while I lived in the suburbs of New Jersey, I had to deal with a bad medical practice. They were the kind of practice that had medical students at every appointment—and while I absolutely support the practice of training doctors in treating disabled people, they never even bothered to present it to me that way. I was a teaching tool.

The medical students would file in to my appointments—routine appointments, for a flu shot or an infected spider bite, or a cortisone shot in my injured ankle—and they would talk about my body as if I were not there. They would explain my congenital rubella syndrome (even if that wasn't what brought me in), they would discuss how my body was different. When they entered the room, I stopped being a patient and started to be a practice cadaver, an object lesson in an endless game of what's-wrong-with-this-body.

Once upon a time I would lean into it, snarking and explaining and playing along. But I got tired of it. I got tired of medical students who wouldn't look me in the eye, who wouldn't speak loud enough for me to hear them—or worse, who shouted at me.

I had been in an excruciating amount of pain for a long time due to my scar tissue. My first doctor at the practice was an older man who prescribed me an unreasonable amount of pain medication. Sure, it helped, but it also stoned me out of my mind, and I spent days in bed curled around a pillow. When I came back to the practice a few months later, when the medication had run out, I found myself facing a new doctor. The old doctor was gone. The new doctor screamed at me, told me I was pill seeking and that no one would ever prescribe a painkiller for me at the practice again.

I didn't go back until I had the flu a year later. I tried desperately to avoid the doctor's office, walking on a torn ligament and remaining silent about chronic conditions that got worse the longer I ignored them.

Disabled bodies are treated as plot points, not only by the medical genre of TV and film but by the actual medical profession itself. The medical system is based on problem-solving, looking at bodies as logic problems, and conditions as things to fix. I call it Diagnosis Capitalism.

Diagnosis Capitalism is the default lens that doctors see through, and while I believe many doctors join the medical profession intending to heal, everyone ends up on the Diagnosis Capitalism train. Why? Because the American medical system is in the business of making money, not necessarily healing bodies.

Once you have a diagnosis, the insurance companies can label you as expensive, the medical system can categorize you, and they can eventually present solutions that fit your particular situation. Diagnosis Capitalism is pervasive because it offers a way to look at illness outside of the context of the doctor-patient relationship.

Nondisabled society really likes doctors. Doctors are revered as the smartest and most compassionate people in the world. We love hero narratives about medical professionals, which often place disabled bodies in direct contention with the system that is sup-posed to help us. By creating heroes out of doctors, and problems out of disabled bodies, TV and film fuel the already adverse rela-tionship between medicine and patient. So when disabled people resist cures, or resist the "conventional" treatments in order to do what is best for their bodies, they become not just the problem but the *antagonist*. And this narrative plays out consistently in both mainstream journalism and fictional medical dramas.

Medical shows are some of the most enduring genre shows on television. There are ten medical shows running in the United States, as of September 2020.[10] There were twenty-four medical shows running between 2010 and 2020.[11] This genre is pervasive, popular, and clearly a large moneymaking machine for television studios.

General Hospital started airing in 1963. Unabashedly a soap opera, it focuses less on patient care than some of its successors, but the diseases, disabilities, and injuries that doctors must treat is still a major focus.

---

10 *Grey's Anatomy, Chicago Med, The Good Doctor, The Resident, New Amsterdam, Virgin River, Ratched, Medical Police* (and these are only the fictional medical shows, not counting reality TV shows which focus on the practice of medicine).

11 The above footnote, PLUS: *Miami Medical, Body of Proof, Private Prac-tice, Nurse Jackie, HawthoRNe, Trauma, Mercy, Three Rivers, Hart of Dixie, A Gifted Man, Emily Owens, MD, The Mob Doctor, Monday Morn-ings, The Knick, The Night Shift, Code Black, Heartbeat,* and *Pure Genius.*

In 2005, *Grey's Anatomy* aired its first episode. Another romance-focused doctor show, this one took a "monster of the week" approach. Each new week brought a new interesting case for the doctors to solve. Their personal lives are the main focus, as they go from residents to doctors, from flirting to married, but the real disabilities (and medical ethics) that face them troubled me even as I enjoyed the show in college with my friends.

Before Dr. Meredith Grey and Seattle Grace Hospital, however, there was Dr. Gregory House.

In November 2004, I found myself watching Hugh Laurie (a personal favorite from his days on *Jeeves and Wooster*) looking more grizzled than I had ever seen him before, wielding a cane in one hand and a bottle of Vicodin in the other. Gregory House was a cranky disabled man who definitely wanted to see the problem instead of the patient. He had no interest in practicing either a decent bedside manner or medical ethics. The problem had to be solved, and it had to be solved by him.

I know a lot of disabled people who enjoyed *House* for exactly the reasons that I don't. They found it refreshing to see a disabled man wandering through a hospital who wasn't a case study in inspiration porn. But I couldn't help feeling that it did harm to have a disabled character so completely disengaged from the process of remediating the industry that so harms disabled people. And of course, House is allowed to be the surly doctor because his disability is acquired, but also because he's male. Try to imagine his character as a woman—it's impossible.

Insurance is a crime.

In the United States, the health-care industry is indelibly linked to the insurance industry. Prior to the passage of the Patient Protection and Affordable Care Act in 2010, it was legal for insurers to deny coverage to people with what is called a preexisting condition. What's a preexisting condition? Um. You probably have one. According to healthcare.gov: "A health problem, like asthma, diabetes, or cancer, you had before the date that new health coverage starts. Insurance companies can't refuse to cover treatment for your pre-existing condition or charge you more."

I was born with a preexisting condition. My mother fought tooth and nail to get me health insurance when I was born and paid for it until I was old enough to deal with that myself. Ever broken a bone? Have a light bit of asthma? Maybe you were pregnant once? Preexisting condition.

Humanity is a preexisting condition.

The idea that billionaires want to make it impossible for those with preexisting conditions to have access to health care is insulting, especially when so many nondisabled people gobble up medical shows like they're candy. These television shows where doctors repair cleft palates, try to find cures for wheelchair users, and discuss the cost of ridiculously expensive surgeries are the best proof ever that Diagnosis Capitalism exists. They show, in stark reality, the expectations of the body in a capitalist social model.

This is part of why I have less animosity for *Grey's Anatomy* than some of the other shows. While the show does look at disability as a problem—and cleft palate surgeries and other plastic surgery treatments meant to "repair" a body back to its nondis-abled and perfect state are touted as important and necessary—they also talk about, and radically protest against, the insurance industry.

In episode 2 of season 16, Meredith Grey is fired from her job for committing insurance fraud. They've tackled these issues be-fore, with doctors intentionally injuring patients to make sure they can get coverage, but this whole story arc was devoted to the ableist and systemically broken health-care system in the United States.

In season 15 of *Grey's Anatomy*, Meredith Grey used her daughter's health insurance (which, because Grey is a doctor, is top-notch) to cover the treatments for a girl with cancer, whose father was an immigrant. In the second episode of season 16, after Grey was fired from her cushy job at Grey Sloan Memorial Hospi-tal, she published an article condemning the insurance industry and calling out health care as a whole. She acknowledges in her article how many people fall through the cracks of the system.

While *Grey's Anatomy* is certainly still built on ableist bones, it is possibly doing the least damage of them all. But it does rely on the stereotypes that we are familiar with.

Of course, the ableism of the genre doesn't stop there. *The Good Doctor, New Amsterdam,* and so many more play into able-ist stereotypes across the board. And that's just the United States. There are some that cross the pond, such as *Call the Midwife*, which airs on PBS and has found popularity with an American audience as well.

What's interesting about *Call the Midwife* (and many other foreign medical dramas) is that it doesn't participate in the capitalist model of the American medical show. Set in England in the 1950s and 1960s, it follows midwives working in London's East End as part of the National Health Service. Their patients don't need insurance; their patients aren't wondering if their baby's birth will put them into debt. They have other worries, of course—most of them are dockworkers and factory women—but the care that they receive from their doctors and midwives, while not entirely divorced from ableism, isn't obsessed with the capitalist need to make bodies conform.

Because medical shows are so myriad and so long-running, virtually every disability and illness gets covered at some point. The writers reach far and wide to find ever-stranger medical cases, which also contributes a bit to the sideshow vibe. Find the weirdest body that you can and put it on display. Your television set becomes the bally once again.

So, when audience members are introduced to a specific condition within the context of the medicalized lens, how does it affect the way they view a real person with that condition in the future?

This is how nondisabled people learn that disabled people are problems meant to be solved, rather than people meant to be understood. The context of these introductions matters. For example, *Call the Midwife* is the first time that I ever saw my own condition, congenital rubella syndrome, portrayed in the media. It might be the only time that people in my life have ever seen it, either—but of course, that baby dies, while I thrive and continue to harass people to this day. Not every episode of *Call the Midwife* successfully destereotypes the conditions they portray.

One of the biggest differences that I've found between a television show like *Call the Midwife* and the American equivalents of medical television shows is the ability to center the patient. While American medical systems are still problematizing the body at every opportunity, *Call the Midwife* often asks how best to address patients.

Call the Midwife addresses disability both in infancy and in adulthood. Dr. Turner, the neighborhood physician, has to call off his wedding in the season 3 premiere because his son has polio. But rather than painting the use of leg braces as a horrible thing, Timothy learns how to use an adaptive device on-screen.

I have often wished to watch one disabled child get a wheelchair and experience joy,[12] or for that matter, have a doctor sign with them, on American television. But the ableism of the American social experience bleeds through every pore of the market.

This is the other side of the diagnosis coin, of course. While it is not good to be placed into a medical box, it can also be helpful to have language. In the fall of 2007 I started to have ocular mi-

---

12 In *Teen Mom 2*, parents wail and fight over whether their daughter should have a wheelchair or be forced to walk. This is more common than the view of a chair as independence.

graines. The first time it happened I was sitting in a history class in the front row, staring at a whiteboard. I think it was a lecture on John Adams, but I can't be sure. What I do know is that the fluorescent lights above the professor's head started to sparkle, and I couldn't quite shake a spot in the middle of my sighted eye, which was clouding my vision. When class ended, I waited until everyone in the class had left. My professor looked at me and asked if something was wrong. I mentioned that my head hurt and we started to walk out of the classroom together. The world was swimming on its axis as I walked toward the two steps that led to the hallway that would lead me out of the building. I missed the step, nearly crashing to the floor.

It would be two terrifying years before I had a solution. I would graduate from college, have an eye surgery that would not solve the problem, go to my first semester of graduate school, and realize that the solution was a scleral shell, a type of prosthetic eye. While there is no name for the exact type of ocular migraine I had, we were able to find a root cause, a solution. It's not a cure—there won't be a cure, because it is not something that can be cured. But it can be prevented.

So often, disabled bodies are not seeking a cure, or a way to be fixed; the people who live in them simply want solutions to help them function in the world. Diagnosis Capitalism assumes that a disabled body is a fundamentally broken one, and that it must be fixed in order to be useful and good. This morality-based approach is why many nondisabled people will avoid the use of the term "disabled" at any cost. It becomes a moral question: whether a disabled person has a quality of life worth living,[13] whether a disabled life is worth saving,[14] or whether a cure is better than letting things be.[15]

Diagnoses can be useful when they are not wielded as tools to make people feel less than, or to prevent people from receiving the care they deserve. Diagnosis Capitalism is what happens when a diagnosis becomes a weapon, or a defining tool. And traditional allopathic medicine is far from the only culprit. Because Diagnosis Capitalism is not only a tool of the medical system but a lens through which nondisabled people see disability in general, wellness practices are using the same lens. Ask a disabled person what it's like to be a disabled person on the internet, and they will tell you that they are constantly told to just try this yoga class, or use weed, or take a specific kind of herb. Go sleep in a yurt, we joke on Twitter. It'll make your cerebral palsy better. And curative culture has always been a part of the package. Go to a special retreat, they told Franklin Roosevelt. You just need to live in a specialized facility, they told millions of people. Just lie inside this

---

13　In 2020, during the early coronavirus pandemic, many disabled people, myself included, wrote about concerns around the use of "quality of life" as a way to measure who should and should not get a ventilator.

14　In many medical shows it is a plot point that people cannot receive donated organs because of a disability or an addiction.

15　The use of cochlear implants as solutions to Deafness are a well-known plot, but they do not work for many Deaf people.

iron lung, it will keep you alive. Iron lungs were, of course, important, but they cut people off from living in society. The choice to retreat from society (but live) or be in society and die feels like a false choice. Until society can separate the disabled body from the diagnosis, and the morality that requires them to be fixed rather than accepted, how can we accept our bodies as whole?

The fact is, all forms of healing are in some way in contention with the body. This is most obvious in the experience of those with terminal illness, who fight battles and are called fierce warriors. But disabled children are also captured in that camp, conscripted into fighting a "war" against disability that they aren't even aware of yet. And the genre of medical drama is enforcing that, and policing it, creating a sense of what should be, and what is an acceptable life to live.

14.

Welcome to the Cyberpunk Future, It's in My Ears

Disability and Science Fiction

One of the most egregious genres in terms of disability representation is science fiction/fantasy. It's heartbreaking, because that happens to be the genre that I write and work in, but it's true. I have spent my career working to undo the eugenicist backbone of science fiction and helping to bring better representation through inclusion.

In 2019, I became the first Deafblind person to win a Hugo Award for my work on *Disabled People Destroy Science Fiction*. *DPDSF* was coedited with Dominik Parisien, with whom I also won an Aurora Award for the same project. *Disabled People Destroy Science Fiction* was a groundbreaking project, giving disabled authors space to deconstruct and reconstruct a genre that has been harming them for centuries—starting with *Frankenstein*—when it isn't pretending they don't exist.

When I was seventeen, I discovered a book called *The Warrior's Apprentice*. The opening pages described a cocky young man with a physical disability participating in the physical exams to enter military school and . . . failing. Miles Vorkosigan was the first disabled character I had encountered who lasted on the page for more than a few seconds, and who had a seemingly realistic experience of the world

And Miles Vorkosigan was, for a long time, the only one.

Science fiction has an ableism problem. It always has.

In *Star Trek: The Next Generation*, I saw my first blind representation. I was small, sitting in my father's hospital room. We would watch *Star Trek* together (both *TNG* and *Deep Space 9*), and for two forty-five-minute segments a week, we would escape the reality that he was dying. We glimpsed a future where he wouldn't have AIDS anymore, where he would survive because they had the science to make him better.

It's that kind of thinking that gets us down a slippery sort of eugenicist slope, though, isn't it?

Star Trek wanted to show that they had solutions for all sorts of disabilities and other problems. So does *Star Wars* and a zillion other narratives set in the future, where blind eyes can be replaced with a VISOR and your damaged heart can be cured with an Iron Man suit.

The message, in the vast bulk of science fiction, is that in the future, disability will have a nominal impact on your life because science and technology will have fixed you. This is *not* the same thing as saying that your disability will have a nominal impact on your life because you live in a world that has adapted to you.

Why is that important? Because the first one is a form of disability erasure.

Eugenics isn't just some outdated racist pseudoscience the Nazis used to kill people. It's quite alive today as a social theory that replicates itself time and time again. It's not only about legal control of disabled bodies and their reproductive actions, especially when applied to the disabled people of color in our world. Eugenics is also a philosophy, a mindset that appears in a variety of places where you might not be looking for it.

Like *Star Trek*.

When I think of *Star Trek*, I don't think of disabled people. When people remind me that Geordi is blind, I have trouble conjuring it, because Geordi has an adaptive device that more or less renders him sighted.

I don't think of wheelchairs on the ship, though there is a wheelchair user in the background on *Discovery*. I don't think of a world in which disabled people exist.

Which is because when we start to talk about the future, we think about what will have changed, and to many nondisabled people, this means that disability will have been solved. We won't need white canes anymore, because we'll have been fixed. Wheelchairs won't be necessary. Deafness will be cured with technology—and we're close to that now as it is for some people.

But what if we don't want cures? What if we want to go into space with a disability? What if some disabilities are actually beneficial in space?

So many nondisabled people assume that we want cures—and to be fair, some of us do. I'd love a cure for my PTSD or for the chronic pain in my back. Either of those are welcome to go away at basically any time.

But my Deafblindness? I was born with it. Am I a different person without it? Most certainly. I don't know who that person is, but she's not the woman writing this book. My identity has been formed around the body that I live in—so has yours, by the way, disabled or not—and to remove it would change me irreversibly. "Disability" is not, as Lawrence Carter-Long says, a bad word.[1] It identifies us, but it isn't a negative. It's a neutral.

If the world were actually *Star Trek*, would I exist? Or would they have eradicated the things that make me who I am?

It's hard to imagine yourself in the future when you can't find yourself there. This is one of the ways eugenics works, through erasure.

The point of science fiction and fantasy is escapism. That's why we have it—to imagine the way that things could be. That's not always a good thing; for example, I'm fairly certain most women would not want to live in *Game of Thrones*. Nonetheless, escapist fiction helps us to get out of our own heads.

Many nondisabled writers assume (falsely) that disabled

---

1 Barbara J. King, "'Disabled': Just #SayTheWord," NPR, February 25, 2016, https://www.npr.org/sections/13.7/2016/02/25/468073722/disabled -just-saytheword.

readers want to escape their bodies and the realities that they have to live with. We don't.[2]

Imagine picking up a book and reading about a future in which you don't exist, or where your disability is the thing that ends the world. Perhaps a world like José Saramago's *Blindness*, where a disease overtakes the world and suddenly there are no sighted people. Or Josh Malerman's *Bird Box*, where opting in to blindness is almost certainly better than the alternative. Both these examples are written by sighted people, and they make blindness the Big Bad just as much as the monsters are. The blind experience isn't just a negative; it's not even portrayed as survivable.

One of the reasons it is so terribly frustrating that disability isn't portrayed often in futuristic settings, or even in historical settings, is that it's there in the subtext, or even the actual text, but it's never *named*. Your romance heroine in a nineteenth-century Regency romance who had a terrible riding accident? She's probably disabled, because no one healed perfectly from a riding accident in the nineteenth century. Your cyberpunk hero who has cyber eyes? Yeah, how exactly do you think he got those?

Adaptation and body modification are part of the disabled experience. Full stop. It's part of what makes us who we are. We learn to live with the bodies we've been handed, and find creative ways to adjust. But in science fiction, our reward is to be relegated

---

2   At least I don't, and many of my peers in the disability community feel the same way. Some disabled people do, I suppose, but I'm not often in their company.

to the roles of evil, of cautionary tale, and of victim. It's rare to see disability included in the world building, or for that matter, as anything other than a convenient plot point.

Let's tackle the biggest AT-AT in the room: *Star Wars*.

Star Wars is the franchise that everyone loves. Most people have seen at least the first trilogy, though many won't admit that they know who Jar Jar Binks is. It's inescapable: the geek series that went mainstream. And *Star Wars* is also intrinsically linked with disability narratives.

The following characters in the *Star Wars* franchise are disabled[3]: Darth Vader, Emperor Palpatine, Snoke, Anakin Skywalker, Yoda, Chirrut Îmwe, Tivik, Saw Gerrera, Bodhi Rook, Kylo Ren, Amilyn Holdo. Honestly, there are probably even more than those (is the Mandalorian disabled because he can't remove his helmet?), but for a mass franchise that tackles disability, one thing is clear: even these visibly disabled characters aren't being thought of as disabled.

Saying that Yoda is disabled probably made a few people respond with "But Yoda's a Muppet!" and to that I say: Muppets can be disabled, too. There is actually a long history of Jim Henson characters engaging with the issues of social justice, and there are guide dog Muppets and autistic Muppets, and so on and so forth, and they are named for what they are.

We never address, in the entire franchise, that Yoda can be read as a little person. Chirrut Îmwe's blindness is a manifestation

---

3 Ada Hoffmann, "Disability in Star Wars," July 28, 2019, http://www .ada-hoffmann.com/2019/07/28/disability-in-star-wars/.

of the blind warrior trope, played either for laughs or for awe, and with a blank, expressionless face that distracted me from the otherwise beautiful story of revolution.

Disability is everywhere in *Star Wars*, but most of the disabled characters in the series are evil, or at best, morally ambiguous (with the exception of Yoda and Îmwe).

Disability as coding for evil is one of the most virulent tropes out there. It presumes that we can tell at a distance whether or not someone is evil, and it codes disabled bodies as outsider bodies.

Take Darth Vader, for example. Wears a giant suit of black armor, has rattling breaths that echo like he's using a breathing tube, can't actually be out of his suit for very long or else he'll die.

Definitely disabled, and his adaptive devices are used to make him seem scary. For more than thirty years, the sound of someone taking a breath through an assistive device has been synonymous with Space Nazi.

So have facial disfigurements and overblown representations of albinism. They've created a coding system that propagates across most of science fiction in film, giving audiences an easy way to tell who's evil and who's not.

Which is all the more troubling when you think about the actual historical relationship between disabled people and the Nazi regime.

In 1939, Aktion T4 was perpetrated on disabled adults, with SS officers shooting disabled adults as a form of euthanasia.[4] The

---

4 Piotr Semków (September 2006). "Kolebka" [Cradle] (PDF). *IPN Bulletin* 8–9 (67–68). 42–50. 44–51/152. ISSN 1641-9561.

Nazi regime had already been killing disabled people for quite some time, but this was their first foray into the systematic murder of marginalized communities. It is rare that people remember that this happened.[5]

T4 was eugenics in action. A whole generation of disabled people were not allowed to live. So you can imagine why seeing disabled people's bodies weaponized into Space Nazi shorthand makes me physically ill. As a disabled Jewish woman, it is difficult to contemplate the number of ways in which I would have been unsafe in the 1930s.

Science fiction has a eugenics problem, and the longer that we choose to propagate these ideals, the more we harm and alienate disabled people from our communities. In 2020, I was on a panel discussing whether disabled people "should" be included in the genre, when of course we are already here. We have been here for a long time, and we shall remain. Disability is a core part of what science fiction should be—a genre that relies on adapting to new worlds, boldly going where no one has gone before. Disabled people are the experts at that.

---

5 At the United States Holocaust Museum there is a single case dedicated to Aktion T4. It is in the corner to the left when you exit the first floor of exhibits. To your right is a brightly lit doorway, guiding you to the next layer of exhibits. I nearly missed it when I went. When I noticed the exhibit, it included a mattressless hospital bed, the wire supports clearly seen through the glass. Few people stopped to understand what happened to the disabled Germans in the late 1930s, and for that I felt rage.

———————

But, of course, you're going to ask: What *about* Yoda? What about Murderbot? What about x, y, z nonhuman example of disability in space or fantasy? And you're right to ask. Are they good representations of disability?

Disability is a uniquely human condition. We sometimes see cute internet videos about disabled pets (look at my pibble and his adorable wheelchair), but those animals don't face ableism. They don't know the difference. When we imagine far-flung space societies, we don't conceive of them as built on ableism—whatever Yoda is, he clearly didn't come from a society where having a form of dwarfism was much of a challenge. Did Yoda ever face a service denial? Was Yoda ever denied accommodations for his disability? Not so much. Disability isn't about the challenges that disabled people face, but it is, to some extent, about how our bodies are situated within the world.

The autistic community has often heralded both Data from *Star Trek* and Murderbot from the Murderbot series as autistic heroes. Without commenting on whether they are good representations of disability, I want to ask whether it is fair that humans must turn to machines to see themselves. People deserve a character that actually connects them to humanity—and while I know there are some autistic people who identify strongly with androids, robots, and more, I find myself aching for human representation across the board.

And not just for disabled people. The nondisabled need to see it, too. Given how many nondisabled people I have met in my life who had never met another disabled person before me, or who couldn't identify that they had, I'd argue that we need representation to engender not just empathy but familiarity.

One of the ways to do that is in settings like *Star Trek* and *Star Wars*, wildly well-loved franchises that aren't plagued with special-interest shelving. What happens when we start to see disabled characters as integrated into the world? It means that we start to see disability thought of by the audience in general. It stops being a shock to see a disabled person, and when that disabled person's entrance isn't heralded by sinister music or the "Imperial Death March," we start to relax our notions of what's terrifying.

But of course, evil and nonhuman representation isn't the only thing you have to worry about in science fiction.

In the Miles Vorkosigan series, there is a species called Quaddies. Quaddies were genetically designed for space living. They have no legs and four arms.

Genetic modification may seem like a thing of the far future, but in fact it's already here. Technologies like CRISPR are already being developed to assist doctors and parents in selecting fetuses that are healthy and able to conform to societal norms. Even without CRISPR, there are tests done during pregnancy to confirm the "viability" of a fetus, which also look for the chromosomal mutations that cause Down syndrome and other conditions. Soon, CRISPR will enable us to make choices not just about whether a baby has blue eyes or blond hair, but also perhaps whether a baby has a form of dwarfism. Imagine if we could select to eradicate blindness, Deafness . . .

That, too, is eugenics.

And science fiction certainly hasn't taken a stand here, either. The moral question of whether or not we should play with genetics seems to end up somewhere in the pile of "It's fine, because it's the future."

But so much of the disabled existence of the early twenty-first century is living within the future that my science-fiction-writing nondisabled peers haven't been exposed to yet.

My bilateral hearing aids are pink and gray; they're also Bluetooth enabled. In fact, they're similar to a pair of AirPods. They stream music and phone calls. They also amplify sound. What's the difference between a pair of AirPods and a set of hearing aids, aside from that amplification technology? Several thousand dollars.[6]

Cyberpunk is a space that is intentionally counterculture. Cyberpunk wants its readers to rebel against the system, to question corporate overlords, and to reject the easy path. Many of the cybernetic developments are street tools. For instance, in Kace Alexander's *Necrotech*, street hacks are a part of the story, and they're used to great effect with a disabled protagonist who needs her tech to survive. Most cyberpunk doesn't ask the question of whether or not corporations are already trying to regulate the technology that supports disabled people.

Spoiler Alert: they are.

A nontechnological, nonprofit example comes to mind first. I

---

6 Some design changes, a bit of proprietary technology . . . But yeah. I
   have questions.

didn't own my guide dog. Your contract stipulates that you don't for the first two years. In fact, most guide dog schools retain ownership of a guide until a certain point in the partnership cycle. While it makes sense (What if the dog fails out? What if the dog gets sick and needs to be returned to the facility?), it also means that the adaptive aid that you rely on for survival doesn't actually belong to you.

In another, more alarming example, Johnson & Johnson had a patent for an insulin pump that required proprietary insulin cartridges. Now, I know that seems not so bad on its face—sure, I buy into the one type of adaptive aid that works for my body and then I rely on that for the rest of my life.

But here's a list of questions you may want to ask yourself before agreeing to lifelong brand loyalty for your medical device: Do you think that company will go out of business?[7] Will your local pharmacy have a deal with the company to sell their cartridges? What happens if a pharmacy decides to only align themselves with that one company, leaving other insulin users to seek a different location? What if your pharmacy refuses to pay the steeper price for the brand loyalty and loses their endorsement?

Do you trust a single company to make sure they have enough in stock, or will you risk the fact that someday they may be out of stock and you need to use a different brand? Except wait, you can't. Because your pump doesn't work with any other insulin cartridge.

---

7 Okay, it's Johnson & Johnson, so probably not, but work with me here . . .

Science fiction should be grappling with questions of corporate culture, colonialism, and the body, but because the genre is too busy erasing disability from the narrative and writing us in as cautionary tales, we haven't been able to ask all the questions that will truly matter to us in twenty years.

Disabled people are on the cutting edge of some terrifying revelations. Who owns your hearing? Who owns your sight? Who owns your memory? Who owns your spleen?

We want to say that you do, but I'm not sure that's where the world is going—and science fiction could be helping us to untangle those thorny questions through thought experiments, instead of testing them out on real people, in real time.

If our positive representation is relegated to cybernetic fixes, to robots and to nonhumanoid species, how are nondisabled people ever going to learn that we are, in fact, human?

Fantasy

While I don't see nearly enough representation in fantasy for accuracy's sake, accuracy is a tool wielded by those who would remove people of color and women from the genre entirely.

Fantasy is, however, where I often see better representation within the ranks of characters—and without all the nonhuman trappings of science fiction. Strangely, the sprawling epic *Game of Thrones* fares quite well here. While I have strong issues with Arya Stark's blindness as punishment plotline, and her eventual reclamation of her sight, I do believe that *Game of Thrones* has some of the best disability representation on television. Tyrion Lannister grapples with ableism in the ranks of the high and mighty; Bran has adaptive aids; Aemon Targaryen has a para.[8] Shireen Baratheon dies at the hands of ableism through faith. Their experiences are satisfyingly full. They are often full of pain, and I wish that I could see nontragic experiences of disabled protagonists, but the level of ableism that they're swimming in feels right for the world that George R. R. Martin created.

It's not perfect, of course. Bran the Broken should have been named literally anything else. But in these depictions, we see the complexity of a wide array of disabilities, without ever prompting the audience to complain that there are too many disabled people in the story.

The contrast is marked because, again, audiences expect to see disability in the past but not in the future.

If there's one thing I would ask my readers to take from this chapter, it's that disabled people will still be there long after it has been "solved." Disabilities will emerge that have never been seen before, because bodies interacting with the world around them are not static.

It wasn't easy, as a science fiction fan, to develop an identity that made me feel strong. Half of the time disabled characters died, other times they were cured, or simply put off to the side.

---

8 A "para" is a shorthand term for a personal assistant for a disabled person with a physical disability. A para might help you get dressed, get in and out of your chair, etc.

I might have been convinced that I was doomed to be left in Omelas[9] were it not for the work of so many other disabled people in this genre, fighting to be seen and carried alongside the nondisabled.

If I had been left to Omelas and "The Persistence of Vision"[10] alone, I may have been convinced that not only didn't I matter but also that I wasn't going to get very far.

But I had so many reasons to stay, and so many reasons to fight for the representation that would matter to me.

The science fiction and fantasy that I read, from Octavia Butler, to Patricia C. Wrede, to Tamora Pierce, to Lois McMaster Bujold, all helped me figure out what kind of woman I wanted to be. It was difficult not having female characters who were disabled to look up to, to have more than just masculine characters to lean upon.

---

9   Ursula K. Le Guin's story "The Ones Who Walk Away from Omelas" is a parable about how the helpless must suffer for society to function. It can be read as a disability metaphor, or as many other metaphors if need be.

10   The only example of Deafblindness in science fiction that I could find. Deafblind people communicate using sex. It's a whole thing. I can't recommend it.

15.

We Have Always
Thrived in the Castle

Defying Ableism to Become Yourself

Every disabled person has an origin story. Mine is that were it not for a bunch of Wall Street jerks who refused to get vaccinated, I would be nondisabled. Some of my friends would be nondisabled were it not for one stray chromosome, others because they didn't have an incident with a truck.

You, dear reader, may someday have your own origin story. You could miss a stair, you could catch a disease, you could make friends with a metal straw, you could find yourself disabled in a matter of moments.

If we stop looking at these as tragedies, and start looking at them as new ways of being, maybe the power of disability stigma would falter just a little bit.

Origin stories have resonance. They are what helps us to understand who we are.

Because nondisabled culture demands that we look at these origin stories as tragedies, it becomes difficult to mourn the cause of a disability without being perceived as disliking the person that you are. Honoring that change by adjusting language is vital.

I'm a pro-vaccination activist. I believe strongly that we should trust in science, that we should eradicate the diseases that disable people—polio, scarlet fever, measles, mumps, rubella, COVID-19—we should attack them, we should fight them with herd immunity and vaccines, and we should acknowledge that diseases are generally bad.

But that does not mean that the result of a disease—a disabled life—is a bad one. That it has less worth or less meaning. A disabled life is still, at its core, a life worth living.

My life is worth living.

Threading the needle so that I could honor my feelings about the anti-vax population, that I could not want anyone else to have to be disabled in the way that I am, and at the same time fight for my equality and the equality of all disabled people, is one of the hardest things I have ever had to do. It was difficult to find the path. But it's a path worth walking.

Disability will always exist. To be human is to be vulnerable, and disability is a factor in physical vulnerability. The human condition is about perpetually changing and degrading as we age—after all, the margin of the population that is considered disabled goes up drastically after the age of fifty.

Society does not mourn the abled lives of the elderly, because it isn't considered a tragedy to simply age out of ability. Which means that it is the perception of *when* and *how* you claim disability that determines who mourns for you.

I fought hard to feel like I could do both—fight rubella but not fight Deafblindness.

———

At sixteen, I thought about throwing myself off a highway overpass. It was on the way between my house and the library—a walk that I would take all the time. Half an hour up and down hills, through Seattle's Capitol Hill, and eventually to the overpass. I'd pause there each time I crossed it, somewhere in the middle, and stare over the edge. I'd watch the cars as they zoomed underneath me and sometimes visualize pitching myself over the side.

I never did, of course.

There were always books to read just one block further, two librarians who were ready to hand me James Joyce, Connie Willis, Octavia Butler, Lois McMaster Bujold. The librarians were, perhaps wittingly, my saviors. The people who kept me from drowning.

With every stack of books, with every chat about what I wanted to read next, they were helping me to stay alive. Because I am the sort of person to stay alive for the next good book.

Why didn't I want to live? Well. Being a disabled teenager is hard. There's no one out there to tell you how to be. No role models worth emulating. When all I had was the Helen Keller of *The Miracle Worker* instead of the Helen Keller who helped found the ACLU, how was I supposed to grow up into a Deafblind woman who could thrive?

It made me want to be nondisabled. I wanted to be like Alanna of Trebond or Sherlock Holmes[1] or just about anybody else who didn't look like me. I wanted to pretend that I didn't need a white cane or hearing aids. I wanted to be fixed.

The first time I read Lois McMaster Bujold's *The Mountains of Mourning*, I felt something shift. In that novella, Miles Vorkosigan, a disabled space lord, finds himself on an errand for his father in the backwoods of their planet's territory. An infant with a cleft palate is murdered for her physical disability. Miles—who is physically disabled—sees for the first time in person what he already knew— that disabled people were being harmed for being who they were.

It's the first time I saw a disabled character grapple with understanding the reality from which they had been shielded, whether it be deliberately or not. The reality that they were not wanted. That's when things started to turn for me.

I started to see my cane as not a marker for what made me different but as a tool that helped me to better see the world.

I started to break away from the ableist systems that had asked me to define myself in contrast to abled bodies, and started to only think about what I *could* do within the context of my own self. I did stage combat and Lindy Hop instead of physical education classes, I swam instead of running. I developed the relationship with my body that I have . . . but I had to find a way to do that for my mind, too.

---

1   Admittedly I don't read Sherlock Holmes as nondisabled anymore. The man is as neurodivergent as anybody in fiction.

It finally happened in college.

I went to a Catholic Jesuit university in Eastern Washington. When I got there, I was like a fish out of water. The aluminum Jesus statue in the courtyard between my dorm (the all-girls' one with a giant cross on the front) facing the all-boys' dorm was foreign. The fact that there was a cross in every classroom, also foreign. I'd been educated in secular classrooms with mostly Jews and atheists. I'd spent my first year of college at Evergreen, haven for hippies and potheads. I'd transferred because it was one of the few schools in the state that did undergraduate teacher certification, and I wanted to teach.

It was in my special education class in my first semester there that I started to really realize I was different. The teacher asked me to talk about my experiences being disabled in a mainstream classroom. I had a classmate who was Deaf, and we would talk and compare notes. It started to sink in.

I was not like the other students.

Activism and advocacy have always been a major part of my identity, and this was only amplified when I figured out who I was in the space of adversity to power.

I decided to run AIDS Awareness Week at a school that didn't allow condoms in the health center. In many ways, while my conversations with the Disability Resource Center had always been about the DRC resources coordinators convincing me that I needed more help, that I needed accommodations and support, I hadn't fully figured out how to self-advocate yet, but I found my voice advocating for my community, and this is the form it took.

The vice president for mission wanted to have a talk. At a Catholic school, the VP for mission is not just a figure for where the school is philosophically headed from a nonreligious perspective, but he is also the one who tries to set the faith path for the university as a whole. If I wanted to talk about condoms, or for that matter, about a sexually transmitted disease, I would have to talk to him, and I would have to talk to him using the language of the faith that I had only sort of been raised in. My father had been Catholic, but a drag queen Catholic. The kind of Catholic who throws rocks and tangles with dogma.[2]

It was a long meeting. We discussed the theological standpoint of the church on matters of homosexuality (which I posited weren't really relevant given that while the AIDS epidemic had fundamentally destroyed my community, AIDS affected everyone—an argument that still hurts my soul), matters of teaching on condoms, and eventually I was given the go-ahead to book speakers and form an event. A prayer vigil. A whole week of teaching about AIDS.

Things like this, where I wasn't engaged in the work of disability justice but where I was engaged in the work of social justice, are part of what made me capable of being who I am today. It was something about finding that I was good at advocacy, I was good in a scrap with authority, that made me realize I could do the same thing for myself.

It was around that same time that my college boyfriend and

---

2 In writing this, there's very little surprise that I became Jewish.

I broke up. I'd gone to England and Ireland the year before, and being there had changed me, too. A summer in Oxford when I was sixteen had been revelatory—bopping around London with a white cane as a teen had shown me independence, and the time I spent in England in my early twenties had shown me that I was more resilient than I had given myself credit for.

I have not always been a likable person; in fact, I guarantee there are many people who do not like me. But it was that time spent in England, and the friends I made there, that allowed me to see that my sharp angles and rough edges were actually a part of me, not something that needed to be filed down and dulled, made prettier for those who wanted to know me.

Women are socialized to be soft, and disabled women are expected to be even more so—childlike. But once I started embracing my sharpness, I liked myself more. I wrote articles for the university paper, op-eds that rippled out into conversations at the cafeteria, that resulted in long theological conversations on my way out of Mass, and that made me no friends in the administration.

When I stopped trying to behave, and started to throw rocks and break windows,[3] it meant that my disabilities stopped being burdens and also started being a part of who I was. There's something to the fact that when I allowed myself to be spiky, when

---

3 Arthur once said to me, "I don't know you well enough yet, but you don't sit at anyone's intersection, you throw rocks and break windows." I took it as being seen.

I started to embrace the hedgehog nature that was within me, my disabilities started to hurt less. It started to hurt less that I couldn't see because I knew how to fight.

I don't think that all disabled people are unlikable; in fact, I think most of us are quite pleasant once you get to know us. But there's something to the fact that one must be a little bit unpleasant in order to defy society so boldly.

Sharp edges keep us alive.

To make living in an ableist world bearable, it helps to find your rough edge and accept it is important. Sanding them down will only lead to misery. I tried so hard to fit in, in so many different ways. I described myself as "only half deaf and half blind" for so long, I hid my cane when it mattered, I didn't wear hearing aids. None of it actually helped.

Because they were all ways of navigating in shame. I was ashamed of being disabled. I was ashamed of being different. The shame came from so many different places, but ultimately, it took root. I tried to evade my own reality. I tried to laugh it off, to be coy, to pretend. For a long time, I would have been perfectly happy to not be disabled at all.

It was only when I started to use the words that fit me that I started to grow into who I was. I didn't start calling myself Deaf-blind until my thirties. I didn't start wearing hearing aids reliably until I was twenty-four. I didn't start using the braille on elevators or engaging with the disability community until 2011.

I started to value myself as a person. To feel that my life—as it was—had inherent value, my body was worthy of feeling pleasure instead of pain. What ultimately helped me to pull myself out of the shame spiral was the disability community on Twitter.

One of the most important parts of developing a self-identity as a disabled person is to actually talk to other disabled people. No nondisabled person can substitute for that. Why? Well, because nondisabled people are part of the problem. It's one thing to have a nondisabled person tell you that they understand your access needs and act as an ally, but it is quite another to sit around with a bunch of other disabled people and bitch about access issues among yourselves.

Before 2011, I could count the number of disabled people I had spent quality time with on one hand. When I started to see more people who were like me, my world opened.

Have you ever been a fan of an obscure book or movie? Liked a board game that no one else has ever played? Spoken a language that was hard to find other speakers of? Imagine that you'd finally found the people who you could talk to about it.

That's what disabled Twitter was like for me. I made friends (and a few enemies) with disabled people all over the world. I made some mistakes and had to learn not to show my ass, but that's how activism works, isn't it? We are loud and brash, and we hope that we can find the way to learn to fail better on behalf of our fellow human beings.

I also learned, from my fellow disabled people, about the internalized ableism I was carrying—and started to undo it.

One of the most crystallizing moments for me was when I got my first scleral shell in 2009. I will spare you the details of how a scleral shell is made, but I can assure you that having an acrylic plastic mold made of your eye is nothing to sneeze at.

I had two eyes made. One was the clear plastic conformer that allowed the viewer to see my occluded cataract, the eye that I have had since I was a month old. The other shell was painted to match my left eye. I watched as my ocularist carefully hand painted my new eye, laying down small pieces of thread to recreate where a vein would be, carefully mimicking the pupil and the subtle green color of my eyes.[4] It took her several days to create, a piece of art and armor that would protect me from the world.

An opportunity that I had longed for: the rest of nondisabled society. I could be like everyone else.

When I put in the painted shell for the first time to go out and see my friends, I caught a glance of myself in the mirror. And my blood ran cold. I didn't recognize myself. It felt wrong, like there was a bizarro Elsa staring back at me, a nondisabled woman I didn't know. And I didn't want to be her.

I've very rarely worn the painted shell since, only bringing it out for job interviews and first dates, assuming that my occluded cataract would be a distraction from the person that I am.

How fucked up is it that I believed a part of my own body could be a distraction from my personhood? But that's what ableism does. It tells us that the parts of us that are different, that do

---

4 I actually hadn't realized what color my eyes were until that moment.

not match everyone else, must be hidden from view in order for us to be accepted by society.

What I have come to understand is that the revulsion at my own face with two matching eyes instead of mismatched eyes was like a form of body dysmorphia. My visual of myself is a disabled body; trying to morph it into an nondisabled one results in a strong psychological reaction.

Abled society is constantly creating visuals of disabled people transforming into nondisabled people as a part of their dreamscapes. In *Glee*, Artie gets up out of his wheelchair and dances an entire routine, before waking up. In *The Shape of Water*, Elisa sings. In *The Theory of Everything*, Stephen Hawking imagines picking up a pencil for a pretty undergraduate. These images are all meant to indicate that disabled people constantly want to envision themselves in abled bodies—but when I dream, I am still disabled. In fact, in my dreams, it's my adaptations that are better: I am able to sign with ease; buildings are accessible; I walk across moors with my guide dog.

I do not dream with binocular vision or dual stereo audio. I dream in the body that I inhabit. Some disabled people, of course, do dream of their past bodies; specifically, those with acquired disabilities. But in all the media examples, only Stephen Hawking would fit that bill.

When I started to realize that I wasn't dreaming of a nondisabled future, but a future where my disability didn't matter so much, that's when I realized I needed to join the revolution.

People evolve. One of the ways in which I evolved was that I stopped seeing myself as working within the system, fighting to change it, and I started to see myself as outside the system entirely. After all, if you're disabled, the system is literally not built to support you; you're not meant to benefit from it.

I became a resistance fighter against ableism. It was a deliberate choice, one I made when I finally saw reality clearly. "Accommodations" were just that; they were given out begrudgingly, not out of genuine desire. It took laws[5] to force nondisabled people to think about how disabled people lived their lives, not moral reality. When I started to think about how I lived in opposition to the ableist society I had been raised in, I grew a little taller.

I stopped being so scared of myself.

I had to get out of my own way. I had to stop worrying about what other disabled people looked like and focus on who I was and what made me disabled. I had to own the body I lived in and stop comparing it to everyone else's. The world will do plenty of that for you. Someone always wants to tell you who you're supposed to be.

I had to put my head down and focus on what mattered to me. Of course, the world didn't want me to have equality, so I found myself on the front lines of the fight, kicking down doors to explain what it was like to live my life, instead of asking for permission to live it at all.

I'm still learning. I'm still discovering more about myself than I knew before. Existing on the sliding scale of disability means

---

5 Read: consequences.

that I'm always relearning how to cast myself in opposition to the world I live in.

There's no good way to survive in an ableist world. Just because I've got a decent self-image and a supportive community doesn't mean I don't suffer. I do. I get hate mail, I get trolls, I am told that I am wrong for being proud. My identity is questioned on a regular basis, and there are days when I need to retreat to keep myself safe.

Developing a self-identity out of defiance isn't something we should have to do. We should be able to grow in beauty and strength, without having to constantly force ourselves to stop conforming to the systems that are already in place.

What I wish nondisabled people did to support young disabled people is simple. I wish they made space to have disabled people in their lives. To do that, we would need disabled teachers, disabled doctors, disabled parents, disabled people in all walks of life, in all places. We would need to create a world that doesn't thrive on keeping us behind closed doors.

And the language we use has to change, too. There is so much ableism at the heart of the English language,[6] so many harmful metaphors. What happens when young blind women stop being the metaphor for ignorance? When Deaf people are not bearing the brunt of the metaphors used for politicians who ignore their constituents?

What happens when the nondisabled people in our lives

---

6 And others. Get me started on French sometime.

become our collaborators in the fight against ableism, instead of the tools of our suppression? For many, it's unwitting. But for every stray word, for every restaurant without an accessible bathroom, for every time I have to explain that truly, without a question, I am disabled, to a person who says they care about me and my life . . . there is a cost. I have to wear more armor.

I long to show my soft underbelly to the world. I am not only the fierce knight I present to the world. I am vulnerable. I wish that the world could let me be both. In addition to wanting to sword-fight, to debate, to fully unload my mind on the nearest target, I also want to sit quietly in a park and read a book. I want to snuggle and mutter about affection.

Nondisabled people have the privilege of softness. They don't always have to be strong. But when I let my guard down, I become cute, I become vulnerable. That vulnerability is weaponized so easily.

I've struggled to find a balance, and I'm still not there.

Helen Keller was always the comparison. Still is. Before first dates, I get asked if I'm Deafblind like Helen Keller. Before job interviews I have to ask myself how Deafblind I'm allowed to be at this new job (this book is more or less going to destroy my ability to pretend I'm not disabled at a job interview, and I'm still not sure how I feel about that).

How Deafblind am I allowed to be? I have to sit with that phrase for a second. What tools will make me seem more nondisabled or less, what tools give me the choices to present the way that I want to?

A long time ago I realized that, in many ways, I control the perception and presentation of my disability as much as non-disabled people do. Like Judith Butler's gender theories, disability works in the same way. I can shift and change the ways in which I am visually perceived. With a pair of sunglasses and a white cane or a guide dog, I present as more blind, because of all the tropes and media enforcements that exist. Likewise if I look straight ahead, even with my regular glasses on; stare unblinking into the middle distance; and refuse to make eye contact. It's become an occasional survival mechanism for me. If I look more blind, people will sometimes leave me alone, get out of my way, disengage.

Deafness is a little harder, but I do that, too. I use ASL when I need to enforce that I can't hear someone, I tap my hearing aids, I adjust settings and say "I can't hear you," even when I can, just a little bit, because it matters. When I speak and don't sign, when I don't obviously indicate my hearing aids, many forget that I'm Deaf. How we present disability to the outer world helps us control the narrative as much as the abled.

I've ended up being comfortable with a certain degree of visibility.

Throughout the process of deciding who I was and how I would exist in the world, I had to confront the fact that it would make me defiant. It's defiance to refuse to conform to the perfect Deafblind image, to only use the adaptive aids and supports that I need, not the ones that suit everyone else. To correct people when they assume I am not disabled.

One of the most important parts of developing my disabled identity, and integrating it into my authentic self, was in the act of protest. Without my activism and my advocacy, I would still be pretending that I wasn't blind or deaf. I'd still be trying to conform to an ableist society.

And I've never worn conformity well.

16.

Cane in One Hand,
Protest Sign in the Other

A View of Police Brutality
and Disability

E mmett, the young Deaf male romantic lead on *Switched at Birth*, is working on his motorcycle; the audio cuts out for the audience. We are in his world, a world without sound, when we see the classic cop car lights, blue, red, and white flashes in the darkness. For a nondisabled viewer, this may be the first time that they have ever thought about what happens when you are Deaf and the police come to your door. For me, my heart skips a beat. My breathing slows. I twitch. I have seen what can happen when the police interact with a Deaf person, and it is not pretty. Emmett does not hear the police as they tell him to drop his weapon (a wrench in his right hand). He does not know they are there until the police are on him, until they have knocked him down to the ground.

Rewatching this sequence, rewatching them cuff his hands behind his back, rewatching police officers literally silence a Deaf man . . . in the spring of 2020, it was like several simultaneous punches to the gut.

Police violence against disabled bodies is very rarely depicted on television, and yet 50 percent of the people murdered by the police are disabled. Most of them are Black.[1] Marcus-David Peters was mentally ill.[2] Eric Garner had asthma, and when he was placed in a chokehold by police, his asthma kicked in.[3]

Haben Girma, a Black Deafblind lawyer and activist, is quoted in the *Time* article "Black, Disabled and At Risk": "Anyone who immediately doesn't comply, the police move on to force," she says. The approach doesn't work when police interact with someone who doesn't react in the way they expect. Girma says that for her, the danger is hardly abstract. "Someone might be yelling for me to do something and I don't hear. And then they assume that I'm a threat," she says.

---

1 Abigail Abrams, "Black, Disabled, and at Risk," *Time*, June 25, 2020, https://time.com/5857438/police-violence-black-disabled/.

2 WWBT News Team, "Family of Richmond Man Killed by Police Issues Demands, Calling George Floyd's Death 'the Last Straw,'" WWBT, June 1, 2020, https://www.whsv.com/content/news/v-570937841.html.

3 Ali Winston, "Medical Examiner Testifies Eric Garner Died of Asthma Caused by Officer's Chokehold," *New York Times*, May 15, 2019, https://www.nytimes.com/2019/05/15/nyregion/eric-garner-death-daniel-pantaleo-chokehold.html.

I am white. I don't have the experience of being seen as a threat due to the color of my skin. I am safer than Black and POC disabled people when it comes to encounters with the police.

But that does not mean I am safe by any means.

Because I am a Deafblind disabled woman, I have experienced the true face of policing, as a victim of assault, as an activist, and as a bystander.

Zuccotti Park was full of tents in November of 2011. The police had the park surrounded, bright lights shining into the park at full blast, tall observation towers jacked up to their highest point, looming with menace. Zuccotti Park had been the site of joyful drum circles, of socialist-fueled laughter, and of many, many arrests. I had been assisting with the protest in a variety of ways, sometimes helping the National Lawyers Guild, documenting with a camera, and generally being temporary boots-on-the-ground since the whole thing started. I was trained for this.

One of my earliest memories is being with my parents in front of St. Patrick's Cathedral on Fifth Avenue. All around us, members of ACT UP were chanting "Shame" in the direction of the cathedral. I was four years old and disrupting Mass in an effort to bring attention to the disease that was killing my father and our extended community.

I was raised to resist systems that seek to harm and that manifest cruelty. My father's death was never blamed on his gayness in our household (though it certainly was by those outside of it) but laid squarely at the feet of Ronald Reagan and the Republicans who held office at the time.

I learned early that the government was not there to save me.

In many ways, being disabled is itself an act of protest. When I exist in public outside the confines of an institution, when I proudly display my cataract, when I refuse to hide my hearing aids, these are all forms of resistance against the ableist system. Visible disability in public is an act of civil disobedience.

But like all good civil disobedience, it's not an isolated act. My friends and my partners are my coconspirators. Those who love me *for* the body that I inhabit, and not in spite of it, are also participating in that action.

Why?

Because being my friend or my partner requires patience. It requires a rejection of abled norms. To stop expecting that I will conform to the society that allows abled supremacy and starting to operate from a place of interdependence and adaptation. It's a subversion of everything you've ever been taught.

If we assume (as I do) that the mere presence of a disabled body on a public street is an act of civil disobedience, then we must acknowledge that a disabled body at *any* political action, whether it be a nonviolent protest, a political rally, or a march, radically politicizes the disabled body.

Which is why, when I step onto the front line of a protest, I do so with much deliberation. I know what it means to weaponize the vision of disability; I know when it matters, and I know what the political implications are when it is visible.

I'm not the only one. There is a long history of civil action in the disabled community. National ADAPT has shut down congressional buildings, bus lines, and more. Disabled people have crawled up the Capitol steps, held office buildings via sit-ins, and so much more.

On May 29, 2020, Seattle, Washington, erupted into civil disobedience. George Floyd's murder by the Minneapolis Police Department ignited a nationwide movement amid a pandemic that would change the discussion of racial justice in the United States for the better.

I've been at my fair share of protests, white cane in my right hand, a sign in the left. I've led marches, spoken at rallies, sat down peaceably during a demonstration, and been collected by the police (but never charged or arrested) my fair share of times. But I had never before seen the level of police violence that I saw in Seattle that summer. I have never feared for my safety or the safety of others in the same way.

In Seattle, it all started because of a pink umbrella. An officer took one of the tools used to protect protesters from pepper spray and tear gas.

I don't wear pants. That might seem like a non sequitur, but the truth is, if I can avoid it, I don't wear jeans or khakis. I like skirts. Skirts and dresses are comfortable, they place me squarely in the gender presentation that I prefer, and they deny people the ability to make me out to be something I'm not (an abled woman).

But on a front line, I wear boots and jeans. I wear a denim jacket and a Star of David. I take out my hearing aids when the signal comes that we might be facing trouble. I carry a white cane instead of following a guide dog. I make active and deliberate choices that show solidarity. The first time I headed up to the Western Barricade that day, I had an anxious knot in my belly. The violence had been intense. Even *I* could hear the flashbangs from my house fifteen blocks away; the swarm of helicopters had been near constant, and every time I watched the livestreams by people living in apartments facing the Western Barricade it chilled my blood. But I knew I had to go. I knew I had to put my white disabled body on the front line, because Black disabled people were dying. Black disabled people were dying, and complicity is silence.

So I went. But my body remembered the last time I had been on a front line at a protest that got ugly, and the fear was rational.

On November 17, 2011, I was protesting in New York City. I got caught in a kettle. Thirty thousand people were out in the streets that day. We were everywhere. Union Square, Brooklyn Bridge, Zuccotti Park: we swarmed Manhattan and we marched and we chanted and we made our voices heard.

I had always been so careful. My time at Occupy was almost universally during the day. I was in a collared shirt and vest, running errands for the National Lawyers Guild. I spent some time at the People's Library. I brought friends tea. I did my best to stay safe, because I didn't really want to get arrested.

But I turned a wrong corner in the dark. I was trying to avoid Brooklyn Bridge—they had a Long Range Acoustic Device out, and that's one of those things you don't want to experience while wearing hearing aids. I couldn't tell you where the kettle was; all I know is I'd lost my way in the dark, and suddenly the NYPD had me caught in one of their traps. Kettled with lots of other activists, waiting to get maced in the face (because that's usually what occurs next).

That's when it happened.

The police took my white cane. They told me it was a weapon. They never charged me, they never arrested me, but they disabled me in the middle of mass civil disobedience.

My parents had raised me not to trust the police. Between the ACT UP protests I attended as a child and the police officers who terrorized the local homeless population in the Belltown of my Seattle childhood, I had always regarded people in uniform with a heavy amount of fear.

This makes me unusual as both a white woman and as a disabled one. Many disabled people are raised with the idea that we should trust the police, yet the police systems and law enforcement systems are also built on the ableism that we experience in larger society. And in the case of American law enforcement (and in fact, law enforcement all over the world), they're armed with deadly weaponry.

As I think about it, 2011 was a bad year for me and the police in general.

On September 29, 2011, I was walking home by myself. This is a thing that I do regularly. Gatsby and I were living in Jersey City at the time, in the neighborhood of Paulus Hook. It was a cute little two-bedroom in a renovated brownstone, down some dark streets, within walking distance of the PATH train to Manhattan.

I've always downplayed the story I'm about to tell. I've always said that it was not that big of a deal.

The memory is clear, sharper than it should be from the power of the way that trauma shapes memory.

I was wearing a yellow-and-white button-down seersucker shirtwaist dress. It was one of my favorite dresses. I wore it until it fell apart. Black heels. My camera was slung over my shoulder because I'd been out shooting a burlesque show that night. I'd spent my evening pressed up against the edge of the stage, cane pressing against my body, my hands poised carefully on the button of my Canon, patiently watching for the exact right moment to press.

It was one of those late September nights in New York where you don't need a coat but the air has an edge of autumn to it.

I paused on the corner of my street. My phone buzzed at my hip. A friend checking to see if I'd made it home safe from the vast distance of Brooklyn. That's when it happened.

I don't know where he came from. It could have been ahead of me, it could have been from behind. But suddenly there was a hand on my left breast and another hand on my waist. I was up against a brick wall, the one to my right, before I could scream. There were hands on me, a face too close and backlit by the bright street light. For a split second the hands moved, and when I couldn't think, my body thought for me. I ran.

I ran for home. I sobbed for the last four blocks, ragged, terrified sobs. I can still feel how those sobs felt in my chest. I can still hear them, because it felt like I was outside of my body.

I think, if my body hadn't taken over, he probably would have done more. But maybe not. I'll never know, and I'm grateful for that.

When I arrived home, Gatsby insisted I call the police.

They came. I felt so small in our already small apartment. I told them what had happened.

Within seconds, it became my fault.

Why had I, a blind woman, been out by myself after 9:00 p.m.? Why hadn't I been picked up from the train by my partner or by a friend? Why wasn't I accompanied? Could I identify my attacker? Could they trust my witness statement, since I carry a white cane? The questions were so fast, and so judgmental. The officers' tone of voice felt like knives piercing my skin. I had never reported my rape, or any other unpleasant interactions I'd experienced. I had reported *this* only because I thought it was clear that I was a victim. I thought there was no way that the police would believe it was somehow my fault.

But blame finds a way.

Less than two months later, at the Zuccotti protests, the police took my cane from me.

Which is why, when I went to the intersection of Twelfth and Pine in Seattle, my heart thudded in my chest like a rabbit's and my stomach churned like it was on a stormy sea. I was reasonably afraid of the people who would be on the other side of that thin metal fence.

I knew that the police were my enemy, not my friend. Unlike most white women of my age, I would not call them if they were needed. Not even to help manage a friend in crisis. I would show up myself instead. I would not call the police to save myself. I would call a friend instead.

So, on the front line at the Western Barricade, my beliefs were solidified.

Another day, another protest in beautiful Seattle. I feel the preacher coming long before I hear him yelling at us. We're all at least six feet from one another, and everyone I can see is wearing a mask.

The peacekeepers deploy, chasing him into the bushes and keeping him away from the speakers. William[4] is a known quantity out here on the protest circuit. He's been up at the CHOP (Capitol Hill Occupied Protest, formerly the Capitol Hill Autonomous Zone [CHAZ] by this point in June 2020), and I know many people who've encountered him. He attempted to pray for me once, and I narrowly avoided it.

Something about this particular protest makes my spine prickle. It's smaller, less well attended than the last march I'd been to out of this park. Smaller protests are easier to attack, easier to quash. I'm at the point in our relationship where I've started to tell Arthur where I am, because I know he worries.

---

4 For Mr. Collins of *Pride and Prejudice*, of course.

I've been on a front line more times than I can count, and every time the shit hits the fan, that prickle on my spine is there. Trusting my gut and my instincts at a rally have, for the most part, taken me to safety every time.

William gets closer. I don't know why he's yelling about abortion at a Black Lives Matter rally, but here we are. The peacekeepers push him back again. Soon, there are more peacekeepers moving through the crowd, asking for nondisabled people to come up to the street. Eeyore and I start to move toward the street where the march will take place.

Whenever they call for "able-bodied" people, it means we need to form a barricade with our bodies. I do not exempt myself from this action, not after the Seattle Police Department literally threw a flash bang grenade underneath the wheelchair of a protestor. Not after the way that the NYPD treated my cane like a weapon. Not after my peers at National ADAPT were carried out of the Capitol building in Washington, DC.

I know the drill.

When Eeyore and I get to the street, we step into a formation. Before I link arms with her, and with the young man at my right, I take out my hearing aids, tossing them into a hard case and putting them into my backpack. My cane stays out. I'll need it when we start to march. This march is less than fourteen days before Summer Taylor is murdered on I-90, by a speeding car tearing through an action holding traffic in place. The threats of car violence against protestors are very real, but we don't yet know how bad it will get.

So we link arms. We create a barricade. Our eyes locked on

the horizon. As Eeyore and I stand, we explain how civil disobedience and nonviolent action work to the people we're with. Some of them are new, they've never faced down the police before. We explain how it works. How to sit. When to stand.

Later, when we arrive at the park to which we had marched, we are called again to stand on the front line, but we are not protecting people from police at this point.

William is back. He wants to go and bring the word of God to those gathered against racial violence and inequality. He doesn't seem to understand that he is hurting people—or maybe he does.

Before my compatriots can start to yell about Jesus being a protestor, I raise my voice and start singing "This Little Light of Mine." Literally everyone on the line knows it.

We drown him out with the songs of his own faith. It's not big, but it's something.

———

I spend a lot of time thinking about how we discuss activism. Most activists I know on the left have never heard of the Capitol Crawl[5] or the 504 Sit-In[6] until I tell them to go watch *Drunk History* or *Crip*

———

5 In March 1990, ADAPT organized a protest where one thousand disabled Americans marched from the White House to the US Capitol to demand the Americans with Disabilities Act. Upon arriving at Congress, sixty people got out of their wheelchairs and physically crawled up the steps to demand equal access under the law.

6 On April 5, 1977, multiple sit-ins at the US Department of Health, Edu-

Camp. Most of them have never seen a blind woman on a front line, either. Most of the time I get asked if I wouldn't feel safer being at home.

In season 2 of *Switched at Birth*, we get our first fictional disabled protest on national television. A group of Deaf kids, upon hearing that their school is being shut down for lack of funding, decide to occupy it. It is an episode which airs with few audio cues and limited amounts of oral English.

The episode was revolutionary. It showed teens like I was, participating in activism like I had for decades. I participated in Iraq War protests in high school. I organized gay-marriage rallies in college. What is interesting about this episode is that, unlike in season 1, when Emmett is arrested, they do not depict the trouble with police interactions with Deafness in the same way. And I wish they had. I wish they had shown what happens to Deaf and blind and disabled activists—especially in the context of what would come to our country soon enough.

In 2017, National ADAPT came to the United States Congress to demand the protection of the Affordable Care Act (ACA), the bill that gave millions of disabled people access to health care. A bill that Republicans and the Trump administration was trying to claw apart, removing safety for us all. At first, I watched from

---

cation, and Welfare offices began, asking for regulations to support disabled people be signed into law. The most successful of these sit-ins was in San Francisco and lasted twenty-five days with more than 150 disabled participants.

a distance while my peers were literally lifted out of their wheel-chairs and carried to vans. I live-tweeted while my friend was arrested, her wrists zip-tied in a power chair.

Soon enough, it would be my turn.

I have spent enough time in the street to know that my body is worth something on the front line of a protest, and that my instincts are an asset to the community when we protest injustice.

But those same people who tell me to go home are often the ones chanting for everyone to get out of your houses and into the streets. They are the same ones who throw guilt trips at anyone who will listen—and I wish that they would think about the tension between those two things. The fact is, it's not entirely safe for me to be out on a front line.

Now that I'm in my midthirties, the idea of my spending a few days in jail looks a lot less fun. I think carefully. Am I willing to risk the mental health of the people who care about me for this cause? Am I willing to risk my own? The action has to align with my values, and the action has to be willing to protect me.

What do I mean by that?

There are many activists who believe that the only way to make change is to create a visual spectacle that cannot be ignored.

There are many kinds of civil disobedience that are needed to topple injustice, to destroy what we need to rebuild. Yes, we need the kind of sit-in where one puts their body on the line; yes, we need to destroy property since the system only prioritizes the belongings of the wealthy. But we also need to communicate with our fellow protestors about what kind of protest they are attending.

But because of my experiences with the police, I don't trust them. And neither do most of the other disabled people I know. Most of us have had bad experiences, most of us have felt unsafe in the presence of an officer of the law.

Which is why it's so weird that media depicts disabled people as feeling safe with them.

In *Hush*, we're meant to feel relief when the police arrive to rescue the Deaf author from the home intruder who has been terrorizing her. In *Red Dragon*, it is the FBI that keeps Reba safe. *In the Dark* even has a police officer as a love interest. Disabled people are constantly told in these films that the police are there to help us, yet in reality that's rarely the case.

We are told that we are unreliable witnesses; we are murdered; we are blamed for what happens to us.

When I see blue, white, and red flashing lights, my heart rate doesn't go down, it goes up.

17.

Hindsight Is 20/20, Except
If You're Me and Then It's
[REDACTED]

How do I end a book about my life when I'm not a finished story?

As I wrote this book I experienced dozens of beginnings and endings, seismic shifts that showed me where I'm going and where I didn't want to be any longer. Everything changes, all the time.

A month after I sold the book, I stood in the middle of Hyde Park beside the Serpentine and wept. I was alone in London, a city I'd lived in before, and I knew my marriage was over. I slipped the wedding band and engagement ring off my left hand and tucked them away in my purse. I would not put them back on until I arrived back in the United States a week later. My marriage would officially end on December 1, but it had been over for much longer than that, even longer than perhaps its two participants realized.

I would get on a plane to Seattle as soon as my classes ended. I would fly home and start dreaming of a new life. I would meet Arthur, I would meet many others, I would attempt to start living a life built on hope rather than escape.

When I went back to New Jersey to pack my belongings, it was like I was on the clock. It had to get done quickly. I needed to be off of the East Coast as soon as possible. I couldn't explain it. Everyone told me I had more time; everyone told me to slow down. But I was insistent; I had to get home, and fast.

On January 1, 2020, I woke up on the furthest shore of the United States that I could get to. I stuck my feet in the ocean, and the Pacific welcomed me home.

On January 28, 2020, I sat in the back of Rye House, a bar I'd gone to on one of my first dates when I moved to New York in 2009. I'd been here ten and a half years, long enough to know it wasn't really home. I thought maybe ten people would show up at my going away party. It was cold; it was dark.

Twenty-five people showed up to wish me well. Nearly thirty by the end of the night. My friends bought me Scotch and hugged me and held my hand. We went to Marie's Crisis and sang show tunes long into the night. I will forever remember my friend Artemis holding me in her arms while I sobbed along to "Another Hundred People" from *Company*. We sang "Back to Before." We sang, and we cried.

On February 8, 2020, I walked the length of Manhattan and I said goodbye. I had no idea that it would really be my last day in New York City for a long time, longer than any of us could imagine.

I didn't know that I would be saying goodbye to my friends for so long that I would start to miss their voices. That they wouldn't be able to come visit me. I assumed that I would get to come back.

On February 9, 2020, I landed in Seattle. I had gotten up at 4:00 a.m. East Coast time, grabbed my bags, had coffee with my dad,[7] and got into an Uber. I watched my last New Jersey sunrise as a resident from Terminal A at Newark. Astra snored on my feet.

When I got to Seattle on the ninth, I was exhausted. Mentally, physically, spiritually. I had so much to unpack. I'd come with two suitcases, a bag for the dog, and a backpack with my laptop. The house I arrived at was on the top of Queen Anne, the tallest hill in Seattle. It overlooks the sound and you can see off into the islands. I stood on the deck in the chill of the late winter sun, breathed in the sea air, and let out the breath I had been holding for several years.

I was home, I was alone, I was safe.

I was home.

Within three days I was hideously ill. Deep-down-to-my-bones ache, a high fever, barely could get myself to the bathroom before going back to bed and sleeping for another four hours sick. I drifted in and out of consciousness for four days and spent the next week exhausted.[8]

---

7 Not my actual dad. He's Agatha's dad, but her parents claim me as their daughter, so this is easier.

8 Since then, my doctors have suggested that I probably had COVID.

After I got over the initial illness I moved onto a houseboat. This time I was on Lake Union, my front yard the water and the kayakers and the sunrise. It was there that I started to write this book, and where I started to reclaim myself again.

Remembering who you are is a process that takes time. The first time that I ordered groceries was a challenge. Thinking about what I wanted to cook for dinner—not what my ex would have eaten—was the big change. Realizing that I could watch whatever TV I wanted. Learning that I didn't have to worry about how late I stayed up to read or to watch something. It really did make a difference.

I started to become the Elsa that I had been before my marriage, or even just five years earlier. I found joy in being silly; I remembered what it was like to flirt over terrible historical references. I played footsie with Arthur while reenacting the Cold War in a board game. I watched so much bad TV, but it had a purpose.

I was still anxious when I had to order groceries. Still worried that I would get the wrong thing, or that I would make a bad meal. I started to forgive myself for getting lost down a path that wasn't mine to walk.

On March 1, 2020, I moved into my new home, a small cottage I would share with my mother until July. I flung open all the suitcases on my bed and hung up every item of clothing. I carefully folded every item that went in a drawer. I shoved my suitcases in a corner. Something released in my heart; I was flooded with relief that I was going to be in one place for a while. I had no idea then how long it would actually be.

I was full of plans. I was supposed to have Shabbat dinner with Arthur a few weeks after moving into my place; my colleagues were talking about bringing me on to help with a show. It looked as though the life that I had wanted for several years was finally going to start.

Then things started to happen—quickly. My mother, still in Los Angeles, had been planning to come back, and just after she left the city, it shut down.

By March 11, 2020, Seattle was in lockdown.

Suddenly, everything I had looked forward to was gone. Emerald City Comic Con and sneaking into a Big 5 publisher's party? Gone. Norwescon? Canceled. A trip to Portland to see old friends? Not possible. Even local things like dates and friend visits were mostly canceled. One interested party had a car, and Arthur was up for visits on foot.

I was trapped.

It felt so unfair. I'd been trapped for five years already. The only times that I felt joy were when I left New Jersey. The airport became my lifeline, the train became my best friend. The ability to walk out the front door was the only thing keeping me sane.

I hadn't gone more than a month or two without traveling in several years, and for the first time I was grounded. At least I was grounded in the place that I most wanted to be: Seattle.

I realized that my life had been built around the travel that I used to get away from my old life, that I hadn't been able to sit down and stay still because I had wanted so desperately to be anywhere but home.

Sheltering in place was difficult. Passover broke my heart. I found myself processing my divorce at the same time as I was processing the second pandemic of my life.

From 1985 to 1993, my father fought the AIDS virus every day. It killed him in the end, just like millions of other people in this world. And the trauma stuck with me.

For weeks when the pandemic started, I found myself swimming through my own trauma.

The days ran together. Dietrich, one of the two men I dated that spring, and I would watch television shows and snuggle his dog. We would go on walks.

There are two ways that relationships can go in a pandemic. I've experienced them both, and I think I understand how they happen. In a pandemic, people are rare.

There are the people who fall in love quickly, who try to create a future faster than you can catch up to them, and those are the people you should not probably stay with. Despite trying, I found myself realizing that what Dietrich wanted was not what I could give—total emotional labor and support. Constant nourishment of his well-being while I tried to keep myself afloat.

Then there are the relationships that grow slowly. Cautiously. Facing the apocalypse means that all you want in the world is for something good to happen, for the world to stop and for it to be just about you and this other person. You want love so badly it hurts—and doubly so when you're going through a divorce. You want to know that you matter.

I wrote this book while falling in love. Arthur and I found each other before the pandemic started, but things didn't really solidify until we took the time to see what was there below the surface. I'm not even sure we were seriously dating before the summer of 2020. We had flirtation, sure, we had a certain amount of interest in one another. But he wasn't the person he is to me today, certainly.

We settled on being intentional, on giving each other space to see what could be together. We let it happen. In a pandemic, that's what you have to do, to water what you want and need, and to allow the rest to fall away.

The book is coming to an end, as all books do. What's weird about this book is that while I wrote it, my world changed so much and the book changed me, too. Because the process of interrogating and investigating media has illuminated a lot about who I am, but the process of writing about my life has also shown me who I want to be now that I live a different life.

Snapshots from spring 2020:

It's Passover. Cool enough that I need a denim jacket but warm enough that I regret the leggings I wore under my dress. The seder had been strange. Singing the prayers by myself at a table midday while my family on the East Coast met at sundown was odd. The seder plate I'd created was a mishmash of traditions, substituting parts for requirements because I didn't have a lamb bone, and I've never much cared for apples. The tradition that usually made me feel whole hung hollow in my chest.

But as with much of the spring of 2020, Arthur was interested in a walk. I met him after dark in the shadow of the water tower in Volunteer Park. We strolled through at a brisk pace, ultimately ending up on a park bench in the chill. Back then he still made me a little nervous. We talked about books and stories and he gave me the space to talk about how strange the seder had been. We gazed up at the dark sky and found ourselves seeing who we were together.

———————

I am on perhaps the billionth Zoom call of spring 2020. It's May 29, and I have just lost a Nebula Award. I was prepared for the loss; it's hard for a small indie tabletop gaming manual to measure up to a video game. A friend and I are discussing the protests she had attended the night before. We are both old hands at activism, and a little embittered. She said it was the worst police violence she had ever seen, and she's white. That's how I knew it was bad.

The very next day I am transfixed by the screen of my laptop, watching as a police officer yanks a pink umbrella from the hands of a protestor, mere steps from the spot where Arthur and I had our last walk. We'd met at the corner of Cal Anderson Park not a week before.

This is the moment when the world turns upside down, though I didn't know it then. My life shifts from full-time freelance to full-on activism. When I am not monitoring livestreams or talking to people about what's happening at the Capitol Hill Autonomous Zone, I am preparing to march, or marching. Dietrich and I visit the CHAZ with Eeyore, taking in everything we can as two historians would.

The sirens are everywhere. The helicopters fly too low over my house. The sirens are endless, and at a certain point I hallucinate them, they fill in the silence when they shouldn't. I have grown too used to living close to a war zone of sorts. I cancel work events, I shift essay topics to address white supremacy. I bide my time.

One night, something truly awful happens. I'm up late, not sleeping because of the fucking sirens again, so I turn on the livestream for the march on the highway.

I tune in not thirty seconds before a car drives through the protest, striking the livestreamer I was watching and killing their friend.[9] I watch as their body flies in the air, as the livestream goes offline. I watch.

I do not sleep.

When Arthur comes over days later, he wraps me in his arms and he says, "I'm glad you're okay." And I know what he means. It's the first time that I feel like I'm really falling in love with him. It had been there for a while, in the first time I gave him a book, in the way that he marked Shabbat with me like no one else has.

———————

Astra stops doing his job properly in June. He steps off a curb without stopping first. It was a small action, one that I corrected, but it signaled something was happening in his brain that I couldn't predict. Astra was bored.

He broke out of the house to go visit the neighbor dog and

———————

9 Summer Taylor died that day, and Diaz Love was permanently injured.

went straight into their house to find his friend. He leaped at everyone, bouncing furiously to lick faces and give enthusiastic greetings to everyone he met off harness (and there weren't that many people to do that to back then). In July, he stopped in the middle of the street to eat a chicken bone. I called my guide dog school and asked for help. By September, it was time for him to retire. It wasn't enough work. He needed a job.

COVID took so many things from me, but one of the biggest ones was my guide dog.

Another ending. But I was still healing, of course.

You don't wake up one day and find yourself suddenly healed from a divorce. It's not like a cut on your leg or a mosquito bite. It's more like a broken bone. It takes weeks to heal, and even after the cast is off, there will be times when the bone aches in the cold and damp. I think the cast came off when I moved into my own place and started to decorate the way that I wanted to. Lavender sheets, a dedicated faith space, brightly colored adaptive aids, vintage furniture, and dragons. The space that I created was mine.

I like to think that my friends started to see a change in me, too. Despite living through a pandemic, despite being afraid for my own life, I started to thrive in my own space. My spine straightened and my joy became more evident, and the world that I had been waiting for—even amid chaos and terror—was there waiting for me.

When I took my wedding band off for the last time in January 2020, I was full of regret. I felt I had failed at a marriage that I had entered into with hope. The truth, of course, is more complicated, because as I learned over the ensuing months, the divorce, while expensive and stressful, was the best thing that had happened to me in a long time.

With the ability to focus outside my own troubles, I was able to see how much must change before equality can happen. The world and how it treats disabled women is still broken.

Disabled women are still disenfranchised in the United States. Hearing aids aren't covered by insurance. Wheelchair users still have to fight to get their wheels from the institutions that prescribe them. Voting rights aren't equal, not by a mile, and the ADA isn't really a complete law. Marriage equality for disabled people? An institution which is barred to those who survive on disability benefits from the state. And that's not even mentioning the dozens of jobs I applied to that had ableist job descriptions requiring me to meet "visual and hearing" standards.

While writing this book, plenty of disabled characters still died as props in major media franchises. I could have added a dozen more properties to the text, and I don't see that changing any time soon. More films came out that misunderstood Deafness and blindness. *In the Dark* got another season. More books by nondisabled people were released about disability. The list goes on; it will for a long time until we do something about it.

Ableism is still threaded through the warp and weft of society. It is still a core system that is propping up a lot of harm and hatred. How long must disabled people suffer under its power?

Nondisabled people suffer it, too. They suffer from the fear that their lives will be over the second that they need an adaptive aid, from assuming that aging or changing will make them less worthy of love. By participating in ableism, we participate in the devaluation of all humanity.

Change must come. Nondisabled people must begin to undo the legacy of ableism in their lives. They must reckon with the idea that their lack of bionic ears or their working limbs do not make them better than the disabled people in the world. They must stop placing literal barricades in our way.

I was enough before ableism came for me.[10] My dearest wish is that society will learn to accept disabled bodies as whole, instead of viewing disabled bodies as lesser than, instead of creating value judgements based on how a disabled person accesses their world.

Wholeness is not determined by how many eyes you have or how many working ears you have. It doesn't depend on which limbs work or how many of them you have, either. Wholeness is about personhood, and honoring the bodies of your fellow humans.

I won't be saying dayenu[11] for my civil rights any longer, I won't be accepting that it is enough to have crumbs. I want to access the world with my fingertips, with my cane, with my single eye and my bionic ears. I want to tell stories about people like me

---

10 The Nap Ministry, tweeted on September 6, 2020.

11 In the Passover seder we say "dayenu" which means "that would be enough." It would have been enough if we had been led out of Egypt but not given Torah, etc.

and have them told to me, too. I want equal rights under the law. There is no dayenu left in me.

Instead of creating barriers, lay down ramps. Instead of criticizing your friends' dating choices, celebrate when your friends date disabled people. Hell, date disabled people yourself. Disabled people deserve to be seen as whole, as equal, and as valued.

In the spirit of this book, that means I want writers' rooms to hire people like me to write disabled characters. I want to see disability in the foreground but also in the background. Characters should wield white canes with joy and accuracy. Cataracts should be called beautiful and not ugly. We start dismantling the ableist system by being seen as more than burdens and villains, as more than the tropes that have been assigned to our bodies.

I don't know how to end this book.

I'm a fiction writer by training. I want to give you closure. To give you hope. To give you that dopamine hit of a story well told. But this story is not fiction, hard as it is to believe.

As much as I'd like to give you closure, I can't. Because I will have kept living on past the last page of this book, unlike the fictional characters of a novel.

By the time your fingertips graze these last paragraphs (or hear them if it's the audiobook), whether it be the near sharp edges of the paper edition, the screen of an e-reader, or the tiny bumps of braille, I will be thirty-six. I will have aged twice over since I started imagining this book.

I'll have fully settled in Seattle, my roots solidly planted. Covered in moss and lichen. Nurtured by rain. I'll have walked the length of my city, breathing in the marine-scented air, trusty white cane in one hand, a satchel over my shoulder with an ebook and a journal stashed inside.

Arthur and I will have been building our life together, forging a new path together with kindness. My friends and family and community will gather together once again after the vaccinations have taken root, the world will reopen.

I hope I'll relearn how to be in a hearing and sighted society. I dread large gatherings now—not because of COVID, though that worries me too—but because the din of humanity is something I have grown unaccustomed to. I wonder if I will ever fully re-assimilate back into the world of the nondisabled. If I don't, I think that will be okay. I am more myself today than I was when I went into lockdown—more of the woman I want to be, anyway.

There's no predicting the future.

I have no idea what will happen. That's why I cannot give you the closure that you seek.

My story will keep writing itself. The ink isn't yet dry, and I am far from finished. That's the nature of a memoir. There's a narrow fraction that you see, and once you put the book back on the shelf, when you walk away from that narrow fraction of the story, the subjects still exist out in the real world in their own lives.

That's what I'll be doing when you close this book.

Living.

Acknowledgments

Traditionally a book doesn't get written in a vacuum. This one got written in one, sort of. Instead of going to writing retreats, socializing with other writers while I wrote about my past and interrogated my present, I hid in a cottage and then a house in the Central District of Seattle. But the internet and Arthur kept me sane.

I was, for much of the writing process, alone. But that was only in a physical sense.

I have a lot of people to thank, so I had best do it properly (yes, this is where some real people's names come in, shocking, I know). First, thank you to my agent, Jennie Goloboy, for believing in my work, and Michael Anderson and Emily Carleton at Tiller Press for buying it, and Samantha Lubash for bringing it over the finish line. Thanks to Kate Davids, Laura Flavin, Lauren Ollerhead, Nan Rittenhouse, and Erica Ferguson.

My team of first readers: Meg Elison, Dominik Parisien, Marieke Nijkamp, Jay Wolf, and the incredible Dr. Stevi Costa (half first reader, half research assistant), all of whom helped me see when I had wandered off the path, and when I was right on target.

Kenna Kettrick, for being the best friend that a suffering author could have, for being my first editor and copyeditor when I started Feminist Sonar, and without whose support I probably would never have written this book.

Dr. Matthew Raffety, who is more my sibling than mentor these days, but who showed me the difference between a comma and a semicolon when it started to matter. This book would not be what it is without your guidance in 2007. I'm so glad that we're family.

Lilith Saintcrow, Alice Wong, Caitlin Starling, Laura Anne Gilman, Seanan McGuire, Meg Frank, Alyshondra Meacham, Mary Robinette Kowal, Ali Trotta, and Adam Rakunas: All were supporters in different ways, some in cat snuggles, in car rides, in text messages that reminded me who I was, in long phone calls listening to me squee.

My mom, Paula, who asked how she could help, dredged up old family videos, and honored that I needed to speak my truth about my upbringing even though it wasn't always easy for her to hear.

I also need to thank my community: Orli, Jess, Kate, Asher, Kathryn, Colin, Miriam, Diana, Ashley, Jen, Avonelle, Alison, Maxine, Ardi. Some of us don't live in NYC anymore. Some of you do. You all got me out. I cannot express how grateful I am for the support in January of 2020. To the twenty-five of you who showed up in a bar to say goodbye, and to the Marie's Crisis community that sang "Another Hundred People" while I sobbed. I'll come back to visit.

And Arthur. It's funny to sit here writing you into the acknowledgments with my back turned and Beethoven blasting in my hearing aids, but I can't think of anyone who supported me more. Thank you for helping me figure out structure on nighttime walks, for letting me write about our relationship so publicly, for the moss, and for listening to me read the book to you in the darkness. These are the writing partnerships that you ask for, and never dream you'll get. I am so lucky to have you as my partner in this world.

It took so many people, so much support, so many hours of emotional labor from my community. The only thing I can do is say thank you.

And I can keep fighting. Because every person who told me that they needed my book in the world made it possible for me to push just a little bit harder.

The world is changing so fast now. It's hard to write nonfiction in the middle of a vastly changing society. But this has been my story, and it's true, and it's real. I hope it changes something. Just a little.